small bodie

T0029877

'Its language trembles on the brink of poetry . . .
Beautifully, dreamily, intricately, it explores
movement, migration and memory'
robert macfarlane

'A book of beautiful and quiet intensity'
helen jukes

'With poetic precision, Nina Mingya Powles shows us what
nature writing can be, braiding place, food, family, migration
and all their legacies. This is non-fiction at its most
dynamic, its most transporting'
jessica j. lee

'A shimmering, poetic masterpiece'
time out

'A river both in and of making, with each chosen memory
akin to a pebble deposited along the streambed'
caught by the river, book of the month

'Breathtaking. Nina Mingya Powles writes with the brave grace
of a deep-water swimmer, the patience and prescience of a
garden designer, and a poet's passion
nancy campbell

'Nina's writing is delicious and so alive, her elegant prose lit up
by flashes of colour, taste and scent'
samantha walton

'Immersive . . . Quietly powerful, this is a pleasingly
hard-to-classify book, as shape-shifting
as an underwater ecosystem'
caroline eden, *tls*

'Astonishing. A book that absolutely swims with
colours and texture . . . Miraculously gorgeous'
the spinoff

Also by Nina Mingya Powles

Luminescent
Tiny Moons: A Year of Eating in Shanghai
Magnolia, 木蘭

small
bodies
of
water

nina mingya powles

CANONGATE

This paperback edition published in Great Britain, the USA and Canada
in 2022 by Canongate Books

First published in Great Britain in 2021 by Canongate Books Ltd,
14 High Street, Edinburgh EH1 1TE

Distributed in the USA by Publishers Group West
and in Canada by Publishers Group Canada

canongate.co.uk

1

Copyright © Nina Mingya Powles, 2021
Illustrations copyright © Jo Dingley, 2021

The right of Nina Mingya Powles to be identified as the
author of this work has been asserted by her in accordance
with the Copyright, Designs and Patents Act 1988

Every effort has been made to trace copyright holders and obtain their permission
for the use of copyright material. The publisher apologises for any errors or
omissions and would be grateful if notified of any corrections that should be
incorporated in future reprints or editions of this book.

Excerpts from 'The Curse' and 'The Institute for Secret Pain' in *Curses, Curses* by
Kirstie Millar reprinted with kind permission of the author and publisher. Excerpt
from 'Bell Theory' in *A Cruelty Special to Our Species* by Emily Jungmin Yoon
reprinted with kind permission of the author. Excerpt from 'Day by Day' in *Tātai
Whetū* by Kiri Piahana-Wong reprinted with kind permission of the author and
publisher. Excerpt from 'The River Bears Our Name' in *Cup* by Alison Wong
reprinted with kind permission of the author and publisher. Excerpts from 'First
Love/Late Spring', 'Your Best American Girl', 'My Body's Made of Crushed Little Stars'
and 'A Burning Hill' by Mitski reprinted with permission of Warner Chappell. Excerpt
from 'How to Let Go of the World' by Franny Choi reprinted with kind permission of
the author. Excerpt from *Whereas* by Layli Long Soldier. Copyright © 2017 by Layli
Long Soldier. Reprinted with the permission of The Permissions Company, LLC.

British Library Cataloguing-in-Publication Data
A catalogue record for this book is available on
request from the British Library

ISBN 978 1 83885 218 4

Typeset in Apollo MT Std by Palimpsest Book Production Ltd,
Falkirk, Stirlingshire

Printed and bound in Great Britain by Clays Ltd, Elcograf S.p.A.

For my family

Contents

A Girl Swimming Is a Body of Water

THE SWIMMING POOL is on the edge of a hill overlooking the valley where the town begins. From up here I can almost see Mount Kinabalu's dark rainforests. I know the names of the things that live among the trees and streams from flicking through Gong Gong's natural history books: the Bornean sucker fish, the Kinabalu serpent eagle, the enormous Rafflesia flower, the Atlas moth with white eyes on its wings.

My cousin Sara and I are ten. We were born just a month apart but she already knows how to dive head first into the deep end and I don't. I slowly lower myself down the cold metal ladder and swim out after her, kicking up a spray of white waves behind me, until my toes dip down and there is nothing there to catch me. I reach for the edge, gasping. I am happier where there's something solid to hold on to, where I can see our splashes making spiral patterns on the hot concrete. From here, I use my legs to push myself down. I hover in a safe corner of the deep end, waiting to see how long I can hold my breath. Looking up through my goggles I see rainforest clouds, a watery rainbow. I can see the undersides of frangipani petals floating on the surface, their gold-edged shadows moving towards me. I straighten my legs and point my toes and launch myself towards the sun.

Gong Gong used to drive us to the Sabah Golf Club whenever we came to visit. He would go off for his morning round while Sara and I went straight to the pool, our mums lagging behind us. Po Po stayed home, as usual. Over many years of visiting my grandparents in Malaysia, I can never remember Po Po coming with us to the pool.

~

I am white and Malaysian Chinese, though not everyone can tell this straight away. My mother was born in Malaysia and moved to Aotearoa New Zealand when she was seventeen. I was born in Wellington. We moved to New York when I was three for my parents' work, moved back to Wellington four years later, then packed up again four years after that and relocated to Shanghai. I was fifteen when we left Shanghai to move back home again, although by then, home was a slippery word.

Where is the place your body is anchored? Which body of water is yours? Is it that I've anchored myself in too many places at once, or nowhere at all? The answer lies somewhere between. Over time, springing up from the in-between space, new islands form.

~

My first body of water was the swimming pool. Underwater, I was like one of Gong Gong's little silver fish with silver eyes. Like one of those he catalogued and preserved in gold liquid in jars on the shelf in the room where I slept, trapped there glimmering forever. It was here that I first taught myself how to do an underwater somersault, first swam in deep water, first learned how to point my toes, hold my legs together and kick out in a way that made me feel powerful. Here, we spent hours pretending to be mermaids. But I thought of myself less as a mermaid and more like some kind of ungraceful water creature, since I didn't have very long hair and wasn't such a good swimmer. Perhaps half orca, half girl.

~

There were pink crabs scuttling along the bottom of the outdoor pool next to my international school in the outskirts of Shanghai. They shone through the chlorine like bright, fleshy gems. My friends and I were shocked to see the creatures here, right under our feet, in this colourless stretch of land where there were no birds and no insects but mosquitoes. The sea was not far away from us then, a dark mass just beyond the golf course and a concrete sea wall. It was always there but its presence felt remote, somehow not real, somehow not really full of living things. I felt an urge to scoop up the crabs in my hands and carry them back over the wall that separated us from the biggest body of water I had ever known, the Yangtze River Delta, and beyond that, the East China Sea.

In the concrete city of Shanghai, the over-chlorinated pool became our sanctuary. It sparkled aquamarine against a skyline of dust. Within my close group of friends, we had grown up all over: Singapore, Beijing, Michigan, Wellington. Shann, the coolest and most stylish of us all with her blue-rimmed glasses; Jessie, a blonde cross-country runner and mathematical genius; and Bex, a guitarist who read Russian novels and Kurt Vonnegut in her spare time, who was mixed like me. All of us had moved around the world every few years, and all of us could feel that our time together was running out. We were thirteen, almost fourteen, but underwater we pretended we were something other than human. Or maybe we weren't pretending at all.

Underwater everything was different, bathed in holy silence and blue echoes. The slanted windows cast wavering lines of liquid light beneath the surface, across our bodies. We felt the way our limbs moved, lithe and strong and brand new. We pushed off from the edge into the blue again and again, diving deeper and deeper each time.

~

On a beach on the Kāpiti Coast of Aotearoa, my dad and I wade out across the sand to where shallow waves lap against our calves. Buckets in hand, we feel with our toes for pipi shells poking through the sand. At the place where the Waikanae Estuary widens and empties into the sea, I stand at the edge of the low sandbank and push hard with the balls of my feet. Cracks form in the sand like an ice sheet breaking apart. At the slightest touch of my foot, small sand cliffs crumble beneath me into the shallow estuary. The slow current shifts to make room for the new piece of shore I've created. I learn that with the lightest pressure I am capable of causing a small rupture, a fault.

When we moved back to Aotearoa I taught myself not to be afraid of open water. There is no sand here at the edge of Wellington Harbour, on the beach by my parents' house, only pebbles and driftwood and shells. Everything scrapes against me, leaves a mark on my skin: rocks, wind, salt. The cold hurts at first but we push ourselves head first into the waves and come up screaming, laughing. I push away all thoughts of jellyfish and sting-rays, the ones the orca sometimes come to hunt. The shore in sight, I float on my back and let the ocean hold me in its arms. Big invisible currents surge up from beneath, rocking me closer. I dip my head backwards and there is Mākaro Island hanging upside down in my vision, perfectly symmetrical and green, as if it's only just risen out of the water.

To swim in Wellington Harbour is to swim in the deep seam between two tilted pieces of land that have been pulled apart over time. Repeated movements along the Wellington Fault have caused cliff formations to rise up above the harbour's western shore. Little islets Mākaro, Matiu and Mokopuna, which punctuate the narrow neck of the harbour, are actually the tips of a submerged ridge that runs parallel to the taniwha-shaped Miramar Peninsula.

Near Oriental Bay, the harbour carries debris from a summer storm just passed: shattered driftwood, seaweed blooms, plastic milk bottle caps, the occasional earlobe jellyfish. The further out I swim, there is a layer of clear,

6

molten blue. It's January, the height of summer, and I've flown home from Shanghai, where I've been living for a year, studying Mandarin at university. My friend Kerry and I dive above and below the rolling waves. At this moment in our lives neither of us is sure where home is exactly, but underwater, the question doesn't seem to matter. Emerging from nowhere a black shape draws close to my body and I lurch, reaching for Kerry, but then I see the outline of wings. The black shag is mid-dive, eyes open, wings outstretched and soaring down into the deep. Kawau pū, the native black shag. They perch on rocky beaches all over the Wellington coastline holding their wings open to dry in the wind and sun. Another wave rises over us and we turn our bodies towards it, opening.

~

Home is not a place but a collection of things that have fallen or been left behind: dried agapanthus pods, the exoskeletons of cicadas (tiny ghosts still clinging to the trees), the discarded shells of quail eggs on Po Po's plate, cherry pips in the grass, the drowned chrysanthemum bud in the bottom of the teapot. Some things are harder to hold in my arms: the smell of salt and sunscreen, mint-green blooms of lichen on rock, wind-bent pōhutukawa trees above valleys of driftwood.

~

The Ladies' Pond is hidden in a meadow in the corner of Hampstead Heath. I go alone to find it one day during an April heatwave. I put my green swimsuit on under my clothes and stuff some things in my purple backpack: a towel, water, two peaches and a Kit Kat. My swimsuit is the colour of green apple-flavoured sweets and the fabric is shiny, almost metallic, which makes me feel like a mermaid when I wear it. When Sara and I used to pretend to be mermaids in the pool, I always imagined for myself a shimmering tail made of green and purple scales.

I pass the sign at the gate that says 'No men allowed past this point'. I notice that the wooden bench where I've left my things is engraved with the words 'RECLAIM THE NIGHT', and I begin to get a sense that this is a sacred place in many women's lives. The sunlit pond is fringed with reeds and willows and blue dragonflies skim about the surface. Lowering myself down from the plat-form at the edge, I launch myself into the water too quickly. The cold shoves air out from my lungs. I take deep breaths with my lips close together, trying to steady myself.

The Heath is my neat portion of wilderness, my new home. I walk in awe under the ancient oaks, collecting red-veined leaves and miniature pine cones fallen from alder trees. Wanting to be able to describe things accurately, I learn the names of trees from the stories I've read since childhood but that I've never seen in real life. The words sound almost mythical to me now: hazel, yew, ash. I look up the names of birds commonly found on the Heath: siskin, coot, moorhen, redwing, mistle thrush, kestrel. They taste strange to me, like made-up words from English nursery rhymes, foreign compared to the birds I am used to: tūī, pūkeko, kākā, ruru, takahē.

The pond seems to contain layers of translucent pearls and blue-green clouds. A family of black tufted ducks floats around me as I become aware of what my body looks like: disappearing, half-swallowed by the deep. Here, there's nothing to push myself off from. I can't touch the bottom, I can't see more than a few inches ahead of me underwater. I am not sure where the shape of me ends and the dark water begins. The only sure thing is my body. I hold my breath and swim out towards the place where the sun touches the surface.

~

When I grew older I looked beyond the canon of Western mythology for myths of women who are neither human nor fish, but both. In Malaysia and Indonesia, dugongs – a type of marine mammal similar to manatees, both of the order *Sirenia* – are linked in traditional myth to half-fish half-human creatures. In ancient Chinese texts there are mentions of various kinds of mermaids, including a sea-dwelling people who weave silk from the fine filaments that hold molluscs on to rocks. In Japanese folklore there's a fish creature with a human head called ningyo (人魚). And we can be eager to attach the mythical status of 'mermaid' to the real world. Ama – sea women 海女 – come from generations of skin divers in Japan. They once dived for pearls with only their skins to protect them from cold waters; now they dive for shellfish while wearing traditional white hooded suits thought to ward off evil. On Jeju Island in South Korea, the Haenyeo women also make a living from free diving. Articles often evoke the women as figures from a forgotten past: 'The Last Mermaids of Japan', 'Haenyeo: The Elderly Mermaids of Jeju Island', 'Inside the Island of Sea Women'.

In the Māori myth Pania of the Reef, Pania is a young sea maiden who swims with sea creatures during the day and rests on land at night. One day she falls in love with a human, Karitoki, who doesn't understand why she has to return to the sea each day. He consults a kaumātua, an elder, who tells him Pania won't be able to return to the sea as long as she eats food cooked by humans.

Karitoki tricks her by putting a piece of food in her mouth while she sleeps. Pania wakes just in time and flees back to the sea, never to return to land again.

~

I was near a body of water when I received a phone call from my mother to say Po Po had passed away. She had caught pneumonia in the night and her lungs could not cope. The River Thames flowed darkly beneath me, carrying bits of the city out to sea. I stared down at the current and used the rhythm of its flow to slow my breathing.

I didn't know Po Po well; I can't speak Hakka, the language of my mum's side of the family, and Po Po spoke little English. Our shared language was food. When we got back from the pool she would bring out plates of sticky fried chicken, aubergine and coconut curry, fried bananas wrapped in paper. She'd watch us from the head of the table, her eyes sparkling. A few years ago I gave her a copy of my first poetry book. She smiled and mouthed the title slowly, tasting the letters, her voice catching on the edges of these English words she knew but hadn't often spoken aloud. '*Drift*,' she said. 'What is *drift*?'

The water radical 水, radical number 85 of 214, is one of the most common in written Chinese. In three short strokes of the calligraphy brush (氵), it forms part of thousands of characters, most of them relating to water – *snow, river, tears, to swim, to wash, to float, to soak.* And there are some that don't directly relate, mostly verbs: *to live, to exist, to concentrate, to mix, to strain.* Scrolling through my Mandarin dictionary app, I find so many water radical words that there could be enough for an entire language of water radicals. I begin to imagine it. It's an inherited language, one I've carried inside me all along. It carries no distinction between past and present tense, nor between singular and plural; as a result it contains all the places I call home, as well as all my memories, and all my names.

Po Po's name, her real one, was an English name: Mary. The name we called her, Po Po, is the colloquial form of wàipó 外婆, meaning *mother's mother.* Two characters repeated: 婆婆. Look closer: a woman 女 and a wave 波. There in the upper left-hand corner is the water radical, a small body of water at the edge of her, one I don't fully understand. When I write down her name, I see I have drawn a woman beneath a wave, a woman in the waves.

The Safe Zone

I am standing on the pebbly shore. The sea is an opalescent grey, the colour of the thickest part of a rain cloud. It is so flat and still that if I touched my palm to the surface it might feel like solid glass. The sky is darkening, clouds circling towards something in the distance. The tide begins pulling at my ankles, peeling back towards the island, all the way out. I can just make out a black wave on the horizon rising up out of the sea. It begins to take shape: a column of black water so tall it touches the sky, coming closer to me, and I can't move.

I don't know when I first had this recurring dream, only that it's been with me for most of my adult life. My dreams intensified when I left Wellington. Now, this dream comes more often than ever. There are minor variations. Sometimes the clouds are black and red at the horizon, glowing with distant fire, the source of which I can't quite make out. Sometimes I'm on an island, and sometimes the sea empties out to reveal a sandbank littered with thumb-sized crabs and small whales. I'm always stuck still, unable to move. I wake up sweaty, my jaw tingling from clenching it.

~

Aotearoa New Zealand straddles two shifting tectonic plates. Active volcanoes are dotted along the country's ridged spine, and several long fault lines run the whole length of both islands. Wellington sits atop a delicate web of active faults. The Wellington Fault traces the western curve of the harbour, intersecting the main motorway in and out of the city, while the Ohariu Fault and Wairarapa Fault run parallel. These split off into a chain of smaller but equally active faults that carve lines down the eastern side of the South Island. The fault line map looks like part of the human nervous system, as if the islands were made of nerves splitting off into intricate connected branches.

The last big earthquake to hit Wellington was in 1855, almost twenty years after the beginning of European colonisation. The 8.1–8.2 magnitude earthquake was so powerful it generated a tsunami and raised part of the seabed, forming the shoreline as it is today.

My whole life, people have said Wellington was long overdue for 'the big one'. Growing up, the threat felt vague, distant. I only became aware of the tremors that shook us often when I was about ten. I remember sitting at the kitchen table of our house in Thorndon, feeling the carpet move underneath me. The jolt made my stomach lurch, like when you tip your chair on its back legs but misjudge it and lose your balance, flailing to pull yourself upright again. I was wearing my school uniform. I remember because that afternoon, the warm yellow kitchen lights made my wool cardigan and thick pleated skirt look a brighter blue, deep sea blue. I remember rushing upstairs to find my mum.

When we had earthquake drills at school, we'd grip the metal legs of our desks until the bell stopped ringing. Now, every month or so, newspapers publish headlines like these: 'Wellingtonians still aren't ready for "the big one"' (14 Nov. 2017), or 'Major earthquake could split Wellington region into "seven islands"' (24 Mar. 2017). When these articles pop up, I feel that familiar trill of anxiety in my chest. In my head I see an image of the shore breaking apart into a dozen smaller islands, drifting out to sea. At the same time I know these headlines are only trying to trick me into clicking on them, and that the movements of the land are far beyond the realm of my control.

~

It was Boxing Day and I was eleven. The pictures on the TV were moving while everything else in the room stood still. Somewhere behind me my parents were transfixed, their eyes trained on the news, where a chunk of earth appeared to move across the screen. I was sitting on the polished wood floor, hard and cold through my flannel pyjamas. But it wasn't the earth that was moving; it was the ocean. A wave. The newsreader kept repeating 'the wave' even though what we were watching looked nothing like a wave; it looked like dark mud, or the colour of wet clay we shaped with our hands at school. It looked like the earth was collapsing and the collapsed parts were swallowing everything else up. What was visible on the screen seemed to be happening somewhere both very far away and up-close at the same time. The coconut trees in the background, those that somehow hadn't been carried away by the wave of water, were the same as the ones at the edge of Po Po and Gong Gong's back garden in Borneo. The palms swirled around in the wind, blurred on the screen. I gripped my knees to my chest. The coastlines of Indonesia where the tsunami had hit weren't that far from where they lived. There was a shot of several kids clinging to an overhanging tree and families crowded onto rooftops. What would happen to them? If someone was taking pictures, did that mean they would be rescued?

Just when it seemed as if mud might spill out through the TV and swallow us up too, the clip cut to a grave-faced scientist, then to a red, green and blue moving diagram in which different layers of colour crashed into each other. The layers represented tectonic plates of the earth, the scientist said, and the rippling blue lines were the moving sea. Red arrows flew across the screen to show which way the sea would go next. The two tectonic plates that had collided were the Burma Plate and the Indian Plate, causing eight to ten minutes of shaking, one of the longest earthquakes ever recorded. I thought of how many fault lines lay between me and my family and friends overseas, and how they could rupture at any moment, without warning.

From there, from inside our living room, we could hear the sea crashing in a southerly storm. It was just over the dunes.

~

Recently a friend who works for an educational publishing house in London asked me for a dream. She and her co-workers were collecting dreams, she explained, to test them out on a new project. They would develop a set of illustrated cards for decoding dreams, to be sold in book-shops and gift shops. Any dream would do.

I emailed her this:

> I have recurring dreams about whales beaching
> themselves in Wellington Harbour. The dreams got
> more vivid and came more frequently after I moved
> away from home. Usually orca, sometimes hump-
> back whales. The dreams begin with them swimming
> close to where I'm standing on the shore and then
> they can't get back out to sea.

Whenever I dream of the harbour, there are whales. I can't always see them clearly but I can make out their dark silhouettes just beneath the surface of the water. In one dream, I'm on a train travelling towards the city along the harbour's eastern side, where the Wellington Fault runs underneath. It's an unusually windless day. A huge humpback whale swims alongside me, keeping pace with the train. In another dream, the sea has flooded our garden and a pod of orca have swum right up through the gate, alongside the giant red aloe that faces out to sea – but the water is too shallow for them to swim back out. I watch them begin to flail. In another, I am visiting some kind of run-down urban zoo, where an orca is being kept in a narrow blue tank only partially filled with water. Panic doesn't hit during the dream itself, but after waking.

~

The 1855 Wairarapa earthquake generated a powerful tsunami in Wellington Harbour, even though the initial fault rupture occurred on land, not beneath the sea. Land on the entire north-western side of the Wairarapa Fault was forced suddenly upwards, tilting Wellington Harbour and uplifting the seabed of the Cook Strait. The Remutaka Ranges, the mountain chain just north of the city, shifted upwards by six metres. In a blurry animated simulation video of the tsunami created by the National Institute of Water and Atmospheric Research in 2008, sections of the harbour flash in pixelated colours like an early Microsoft screensaver. A British-accented scientist narrates the movement of the land and sea in a soothing monotone. The colours on-screen are just like those I saw on the news on Boxing Day in 2004. The digital blue sea changes to bright aquamarine as the tide gets sucked out into the Cook Strait, then floods rapidly back in. Lowland parts of Lyall Bay, Evans Bay and the Miramar Peninsula turn yellow, orange, then red, rendered underwater in fluorescent waves of colour.

These days there are pale blue lines painted all along the coastal streets of Wellington, marking the end of the evacuation zone and the beginning of the safe zone.

~

If 'the big one' came, I knew where we would need to run. The track that leads up the hill behind Kōwhai Street is rocky and steep. Libby and I walked up there every weekend. We were sixteen, it was nearly the summer holidays. The track wound up the hill, each turn marked by a wooden bench patterned with bird droppings and dried moss. This is where we sat to get our breath back while our pulses thumped in our ears then slowed down to match the rhythm of the tide rushing in and out far below. We looked out over the bay where our homes stood toy-sized and perfect at the edge of the shingle beach. Too small to see anyone in the windows, which were metallic black, glinting in the sun.

The salt-smell was receding, replaced by dried grass and eucalyptus and a fresh, wet greenness. We pushed our bodies further up the track, deeper into the bush where the whekī – tree ferns – got bigger, curving above us in a frilled canopy. Now we were in shadow. Gorse as tall as our shoulders lined the track, the ghost-white shapes of spider nests woven tightly between bunches of thorns. When we were little we used to dare one another to prod the silvery webs with the end of a stick, screwing our eyes shut, then screaming.

Once, Libby walked up the track by herself and saw a baby ruru at dusk, perched on a branch. Its mother must have been nearby, hidden in the dark trees. I have never seen one, though all over Wellington you can hear them softly hooting through the night; their name comes from the call they make. She described it to me the next day. The little owl had reddish-brown breast feathers and yellow eyes. It didn't make a sound while it watched her, though she heard its two-tone call later, on her way home. The light was purple, she said.

At the top of the ridge, the ferns thinned out and hot sun stung our faces. We were standing in a sea of gold, the entire hillside coated in yellow gorse flowers in full bloom. The sun had already cast a rosy pink pattern on Libby's pale shoulders so we sat down on a bench high above the sea to reapply sunscreen. The slight curve of the earth was just visible from up here, or I might have been imagining it. I rubbed cold cream into Libby's skin and I could see blurred outlines of the South Island's snowy mountains, rising in a shade of blue a little deeper than the waves, shimmering like a mirage. But then, unable to stop it, my brain conjured up images of the sea flooding in over the tops of all the miniature houses and gardens and cars parked in driveways.

Every weekend Libby and I wandered between each other's homes to make chocolate chip waffles and watch old episodes of *Grey's Anatomy* and *Friends* on DVD. We were in the kitchen at my house and it was unusually dark, the room lit only by the soft glow of the pantry light. I was loading plates into the dishwasher when the floor jolted sideways underneath me. The walls did the same, though it was in the floorboards touching my feet that I felt the tremor, and in the cold countertop, which I gripped with both hands as it moved. The house juddered in a single, symphonic creak, as if all the pieces of the kitchen were fastened together by a series of squeaking hinges with Libby and I at its centre, holding our breath.

Though my body reacted with fear as I clung to the doorway, it wasn't during the earthquake itself that I began to panic, but in the silence afterwards. I called out to the dog, Toby, waiting for aftershocks I felt sure were coming. I heard Dad's thudding footsteps on the stairs, his handheld radio already switched on for updates. 'I'll just listen out in case of any warnings,' Dad said in a casual voice, though I could hear his concern. It probably wasn't necessary, but we knew that large quakes could feel small from far away, and that waves could travel great distances.

Once my hands had stopped shaking and there had been no more tremors for at least ten minutes, I walked Libby to the gate and heard Toby settling back down on his blanket by the door, shuffling sleepily, unbothered by what had just occurred. A ruru resumed its gentle hooting in the stillness. I went to bed and tried to sleep.

~

In her memoir *Birds Art Life*, Kyo Maclear writes of her experience of something called 'anticipatory grief', a term I hadn't come across before, and which aptly describes my own experience of anxiety:

> Anticipatory grief, I was surprised to learn, demanded a different image, a more alert posture. My job was to remain standing or sitting, monitoring all directions continually [. . .] I was on the lookout, scouring the horizon from every angle, for doom.

Growing up with frequent tremors in a city where houses shift and creak in the wind, I developed a kind of immediate physical tolerance for earthquakes. In the moment itself I feel fear, but it's intensely physical, centred in my shaking legs and hands and in my chest. Deep panic sets in only in the quiet moments afterwards, in the echo of the quake. I'm always less afraid of what's happening now than of what might happen yet.

Living in close proximity to the sea, my body somehow accepted the fact that I couldn't constantly fear earthquakes and tsunami – otherwise I wouldn't be able to function. Our house is well within the tsunami risk zone, the portion of the coast coloured bright red on the map, but when I'm home, I'm enclosed in a net of warmth and safety. From inside, I can see the sea. I can hear the wind creaking and moaning in the walls. I'm safe in the knowledge that I can grab the dog and run, if I need to. It was only when I left – when I moved to a flat in the hills above Wellington, or later, when I moved to Shanghai, then to London – that my feelings of anticipatory grief became real and almost constant. To fear catastrophic events when you live in a geologically volatile place could be seen as a partly rational fear. But to visualise these events obsessively, every day, when you don't actually live there, and not for yourself but for your distant loved ones, is not.

~

My mum gave me an old photograph with the words 'Summer 1998, Toronto' scrawled on the back in her looped handwriting. I must be five or six in the photo. It might have been taken by a stranger, or my uncle Peter or aunt Tina, with whom we'd stayed on that trip. They didn't do a very good job; the angle is strange, with both my parents standing on either side of me, looking away from the camera. We're at Marineland in Niagara Falls, Ontario, and the colours have that hazy, dreamlike depth of super-saturated film. The deep green trees pop out of the frame, as do my sparkly pink jelly sandals. I'm clutching my brand-new inflatable orca toy, and my new orca fairy wand pokes out of the top of my dad's backpack. Moments after this picture was taken, I remember meeting Jellybean, the orca mascot of Marineland. You could get photos with him at the entrance to Friendship Cove. He would put his soft flipper around you and try to give the thumbs up to the camera, which didn't work, since he had no thumbs. The glittering archway he stood underneath was decorated with smiling dolphins swimming in spirals.

In the arena, I was so excited to see the whales I slipped and cut my knee on the concrete. A park attendant presented me with an orca-patterned Band-Aid. Two whales leapt out of the pool in unison, a perfect arc in the air above their trainer. They seemed to be flying.

My obsession with orca took new form in a creative writing class during my final year of university in Wellington. My classmates politely critiqued the pieces I turned in, which had taken a dark turn. After watching the documentary *Blackfish*, released that year, 2013, I fell into a deep Internet rabbit hole researching recent deaths of orca in captivity in North America and Europe, of which there were many.

It's widely known that orca in captivity live only a fraction of their natural lifespan. There are many recorded instances of captive orca attacking their trainers, whereas wild orca are not known to show any aggression towards humans. In the 1960s and '70s, wild orca were mainly taken into captivity from the waters of Alaska, British Columbia and Iceland, using brutal methods to separate valuable young calves from their mothers. When the wild capture of whales became illegal, advanced breeding programmes were developed in the US. SeaWorld began phasing out its breeding programme in 2016, and live marine mammal shows are now illegal in many countries including Canada, but the reported numbers of whales still in captivity around the world vary dramatically. The wildlife charity Whale and Dolphin Conservation reported in 2019 that there were still at least sixty known orca in captivity around the world. According to their data, there are twenty-one captive orca in the US marine parks and sixteen in marine parks in China.

I wrote about the whales as if the world somehow still needed convincing of these well-researched facts when, really, what troubled me was my own complicity and ignorance – that, as a child, I had been happily obsessed with the mascots at Marineland. I had orca soft toys, orca bath toys and a special set of Lisa Frank orca stickers. Most influential was probably the Disney Channel spin-off series of *The Little Mermaid* that ran in the mid-'90s, in which Ariel befriends a cute baby orca named Spot. I felt guilty that my parents had, like many others, brought their child to see the spectacle of giant cetaceans performing in time to pop music, and that throughout most of the past decade this practice continued largely without issue until a slightly sensational documentary was made. I was trying to write my way out of this vague anxiety and guilt. But this was a particular type of guilt that was not useful to anyone. I was also trying to write my way out of my recurring dreams: glass tanks, shallow waters, blue walls.

The American poet Rena Priest has written about the famous orca Tokitae, who was captured off the coast of Washington state along with six other calves in 1970, at the height of the marine entertainment industry. The whales were taken from the Southern Resident orca population, now endangered. At Miami Seaquarium, Tokitae was renamed Lolita. She lived for ten years with another orca named Hugo, who died in 1980; since then, she has lived alone in the same tank at the park. The word for *killer whale* in the poet's indigenous language, the Lummi language, means *our relations under the sea*. Priest describes buying a ticket to the Seaquarium to see Tokitae, and the scene resembles one of my dreams: 'She swam close – right up against the wall – and stayed there, suspended at the surface [. . .] I was alone with her. I sang her a song, and she made vocalisations back to me.'

The same year I wrote about the orca, I'd received counselling for mild post-traumatic stress disorder after two men broke into my flat in Newtown and threatened me with what turned out to be a fake gun. I was unharmed; my flatmate's laptop was stolen. The incident is more surreal than terrifying to think of now, partly because my brain can only recall it in patchy, disconnected images. The frosted pane of glass set into the door, through which I could see a shadowy figure; the dark pink swirling pattern of my IKEA duvet cover. In the wake of the break-in I had nightmares involving the same set of events, but rather than casting myself as the victim I was a helpless bystander, watching while someone close to me went through the ordeal instead. The dreams always took place in various deserted public spaces around Wellington – at the top of the botanic gardens, in the empty bus station, in the car park of the museum – tinged with a dark orange apocalyptic light. The counsellor at the student health clinic taught me a basic cognitive behavioural therapy technique to help keep my thoughts from spiralling. She told me to touch each of my fingertips to my thumb, gently, in a slow rhythm, while counting at the same time. I learned to time my breathing according to the rhythm I created with each touch. *One, two, three, four, five.*

A few weeks before the break-in I'd just got home from class, my backpack still on and my keys still in my fist, when the charcoal carpet tilted up towards my face. I made an involuntary sound, an animal yelp. I didn't know what was happening. I lost my balance but landed on my knees on the faux sheepskin rug while the room moved sideways around me. I crawled under the dining table, which was being jostled but hadn't yet tipped over, and gripped the table legs. I remember being more shocked than afraid – *did the floor really just rise up or did I fall down, or both?* – until the shaking went on longer than I'd ever felt before and the thought came: *this must be it.* I reached around into my bag's front pocket for my phone; sent texts to my flatmate, who I knew was especially scared of earthquakes; to my mum, who was at work; and to my dad, who was having lunch somewhere on Cuba Street. People always said that was where you really wouldn't want to be in an earthquake. I knew I should try to reach them before the phone networks went down, if it got worse. Dad replied the quickest: 'Under the table. All fine.'

When the shaking subsided I wiped my nose on my sleeve. I didn't realise I'd been crying, but then, I always cry when I'm scared. I went to my room, where my bookcase had toppled over, leaving a sea of unharmed poetry books. Dad managed to get through the traffic to pick me up from Newtown and we drove slowly around the harbour. It was a Friday afternoon, and as it started to emerge that no one had been seriously injured in the magnitude-6.5 quake, Wellington enthusiastically kicked into low-key civil defence emergency mode, which really meant that office workers went home early for the weekend and people popped to the supermarket to stock up on bottled water and tinned spaghetti. There had been slips around the north-east of the South Island, where the quake was centred, but thankfully our route home was clear for now. The car's shock-absorbers took most of the aftershocks, but I saw street lamps wavering out the window as the asphalt rippled softly beneath them.

~

Most of the time, I'm in the safe zone. But my thoughts often feel like a web of connected fault lines, each small rupture causing another, bigger rupture. I can't control their spread. I feel an intense pressure in the centre of my chest and my breathing turns into gasping.

Like many, I have trouble describing my anxiety. In Mandarin, *to worry* or *to be anxious* is: dānxīn 担心. The first word in the two-character phrase, 担 dān, means *to shoulder* or *to carry*, and originally had the more specific meaning *to carry on a shoulder pole*. I picture myself trying and failing to carry buckets of water, one at each end of the pole, water sloshing over the brim. The second character is a heart: 心 xīn. It helps me to think of my anxiety in such visual terms. I picture a heart carrying too much inside, fit to burst, overflowing at the slightest touch.

My mother is the type of person who is good at channelling worry into practical action and preparedness. In her house, an unused bathtub is filled with supersized bottles of purified water, for emergencies. The bedrooms have packets of crackers and canned food under the bed. A set of pre-packed 'go-bags' filled with water bottles, batteries and first-aid kits wait untouched next to the coat stand by the front door.

This has always stirred a combination of amusement, comfort and panic in me. While she places extra batteries and tinned peaches around the house at regular intervals, my brain flips into overdrive. The scene from my dream replays itself over and over at varying speeds. I see the black wave. I see the trees buckle and break, the glass shatter, the roof tiles bend.

~

In 2016, a deep earthquake beneath the Kermadec Islands caused 'ghost quakes' to pop up on the GeoNet online map of Aotearoa. Ghost quakes appear when sensors pick up readings from seismic energy that has travelled many hundreds of kilometres from the epicentre of a deep, strong earthquake. 'The strength of the quake registers as locally generated earthquakes', according to the automatic sensors, as GeoNet seismologist John Ristau explains in an article with the excellent headline, 'Ghost quakes: The ghost chips of earthquakes'. It's like a translation error, but in the language of tectonics. A large quake occurs and generates vast seismic energy, tricking sensors hundreds of kilometres away, which in turn (mis)translate the shock waves into small, imagined earthquakes.

I was in my dorm room at my university in Shanghai on 13th of November, 2016, when the words 'magnitude 7.8' appeared at the top of my Twitter feed, followed by a tsunami evacuation warning for all coastal areas of central Aotearoa. I sent WeChat messages to my parents and refreshed the page over and over while I imagined the tide dropping away in the dark. Mum and Dad piled the dog into the back of the car and drove a short way up Kōwhai Street, their radio switched on in the unsettled night. I kept thinking I could hear the windows rattling, or that I could feel faint tremors in my six-storey building. What was happening felt like the ghost quake caused by distant, imaginary shock waves of the real earthquake that was unfolding on my laptop screen, thousands of miles away.

A long way south, four-metre waves came unseen in the night, pushing kelp and crabs up onto the land but harming no one. In some places along the coast of Kaikōura, the seabed lifted up by two metres. The words I heard broadcast on the Radio New Zealand live-stream chimed inside my head for days. 'Do not go anywhere near water.' The warning was lifted two hours later, but the islands kept shifting.

An aerial photograph circulated online of two cows and a calf stranded on a grassy islet after their hillside paddock almost completely collapsed. The stranded cows went viral; 'please save the cows I don't think the nz people could take it if they die,' a stranger tweeted.

I left my bedside light on that whole night, my pink lamp casting everything in a peachy glow. I couldn't sleep, haunted by the stranded cows, who mercifully were saved by their farmer the next day. He used a shovel to dig them a path to safer land.

~

Shortly after Christmas, a small box arrived in the post. Inside was a deck of colourfully illustrated cards, with a handwritten note from my friend that read: 'Thank you for your dream.' I flicked through them, not necessarily thinking that they would be of any use to me. While I do believe in the emotional significance of my dreams, I've never paid much attention to anyone else's interpretations of them. Nonetheless, I was curious. I found the 'water' card: 'Water is a symbol of your emotional state, with associations of change and flow [. . .] a water dream may suggest you'll pass into a new phase.'

I liked that the cards were written in a direct, sympathetic tone, while retaining an irritating air of vagueness. The 'disaster' card, the only other card that interested me, was illustrated with a wave washing over a small city in the style of Hokusai's *Great Wave*. In the background was a red sun, an erupting volcano, and a fiery aeroplane spiralling to the ground.

> Dreaming of any kind of disaster, whether natural (earthquake, flood, fire) or man-made (explosion, bomb, accident) can be extremely unsettling. However, such dreams are not typically precognitive. They are more likely to suggest fears or anxieties, or something that you feel is out of your control.

For the first time in a long time, I double-click on a file on my laptop titled 'Dream Diary'. I haven't updated it since last year, when I did a poetry workshop where one requirement was to keep a dream diary for the duration of the course. It's unsettling, scrolling through a catalogue of my own barely remembered dreams. Most were recorded while half-asleep in the moments after waking, just before the dream faded beyond my reach. They're both familiar and strange, as if they belong to someone else ('a giant tabby cat that looked like a person wearing a cat costume', I wrote on the 5th of February). Forcing myself to keep a dream diary often caused entirely different dreams from long ago to rise to the surface without warning:

12/2/19
A small cottage by the sea. Orca dying on their sides, their huge black bodies sliding past. I bought oranges from the side of the road. Recalling this has made me remember another, different dream – just flashes of it. A huge, dark room made of glass, orca kept in blue tanks.

~

It's a damp, overcast morning in November. I'm visiting home after having been away for a year in Shanghai. As I gaze out the window at the sea, a tiny dark shape disturbs the glare. I squint into the light but it's gone. Then, a tall black fin cuts close to the northern tip of Mākaro Island. It disappears – my breath stops – then reappears a few metres away, along with another, smaller fin. I grab my shoes and wrench the sliding door open. I fix my eyes on the water, running hard. A third dorsal fin rises, this time attached to the shape of a curved body. Cold salt-wind bites into my chest as I run to the shore and there's a fourth, fifth, sixth, maybe eight of them now, and I'm running to keep up with them as they glide out towards the harbour mouth like birds in formation. I see a small tail flicking up sea foam to reveal a snow-white belly. A calf swimming alongside its mother. A passing ferry cuts its engine, and then I can hear them. I can hear the soft whooshing sound of them breathing air through their blowholes, trailing miniature clouds of water vapour above the surface as they go. There are shouts of 'whoa!' and 'oh!' from further along the beach, where dog walkers have stopped to watch. I keep running and I'm laughing but my laughter is being eaten up by the wind. I run until they're just a cluster of shadowy shapes in the distance. I keep looking long after they've gone, long after they've slipped out of the harbour into the Cook Strait, maybe heading south into the Sounds, or maybe even further out towards the Subantarctic Islands, far beyond where I can see them.

Where the Kōwhai Blooms

WIND SHAKES THE flower clusters of the kōwhai in my parents' garden by the sea. Fallen petals scatter in the grass next to the lemon tree, where lemons tremble and drop, creating a carpet in varying shades of yellow and gold. The smell and the colour of this corner of the garden is overwhelming.

~

Kōwhai – *yellow*. The blooms of the kōwhai tree are, unofficially, New Zealand's national flower. Pronounced *koh-fai*, but the *oh* is much softer than *f*. Your teeth just gently touch your bottom lip in order to make the sound. As you say the name of the tree it dissolves into air.

~

I imagine the tree often. I see many different versions of it: at night, shaking in the wind, or bursting with new, gigantic flowers, or trembling from the movement of tūī brushing past in flight. The torpedo-like tūī are black and sleek, a white pom-pom tuft at their necks, and iridescent blue-green feathers on their bellies.

~

I moved to London in 2018 to be with the person I loved, whom I'd met the previous year in Shanghai. After months of looking, my first job in London was at a Chinese community centre in the northern outskirts of the city. I spent my days helping organise Chinese cooking work-shops at English schools. On my lunch breaks, I'd wander the wide, suburban streets of Bounds Green, where tall hollyhocks and foxgloves swayed in neat gardens. It was the 13th of April, 2018, and it was 'the hottest April day in sixty years'. That's what people kept saying, emphasising each word as they said so. The phrase spun around in my head like a line from a song.

~

This is where I begin: with a kōwhai tree in a garden in suburban London during an April heatwave. I don't know how to continue; the sight was too much for me, too unreal. So, I begin again with the unseasonable April heat. Sweat on my neck, white sun in my eyes. The pavement was too hot to touch and covered in magnolia petals, crumpled and browning at the edges but still pink like slices of meat.

~

The New Zealand Department of Conservation lists the kōwhai's status as no longer endangered but 'at risk' and protected, like all native trees and plants. Kōwhai grow all over the hills and coasts of Wellington, heralding the end of winter and the beginning of spring. They shed their gold on the street corners and in the front gardens where I grew up. The exact colour of the bell-shaped petals, dark yellow like melted butter, is for me so deeply entwined with memories of my parents' house by the sea and the sunlit garden behind it that I did not imagine a kōwhai could grow elsewhere, let alone here, on the diagonally opposite corner of the planet, where the seasons are upside down.

~

In the gift shop of the Royal Academy of Arts in London, I find an enormous book with glossy illustrations: *Joseph Banks' Florilegium: Botanical Treasures from Cook's Voyage.*

I flip to the index, scanning for K: kōwhai. It's not there, but I flip through the pages looking for yellow. It has been indexed under its other name, *Sophora tetraptera*: four-winged fruit. Kōwhai seeds were first brought to England from Aotearoa by the botanist Sir Joseph Banks on James Cook's first voyage, in 1769. The historian W.R.B. Oliver notes that Banks collected more than sixty plant specimens, including kōwhai, at the very place where Cook and his crew first set foot in Aotearoa, at Tūranganui-a-Kiwa / Poverty Bay, on the east coast. Their landing was not a peaceful one. Nine Māori people were shot dead by the crew of the *Endeavour*, including Te Maro, a leader of the Ngāti Oneone people.

Drawing from the crew's diaries, Joseph Angus Macky records that after examining the bodies of the dead the botanists collected flowers:

> The boats returned to the ship at 6 p.m. Parkinson mentions that some members of the party shot some ducks of a very large size, and that Banks and Solander gathered a variety of curious plants in flower.

~

In 1774, the seeds collected by Banks were planted at Chelsea Physic Garden in London, then known as the

Apothecaries Garden. A writer in a 1791 issue of *Curtis's Botanical Magazine* describes the tree:

> A finer sight can scarcely be imagined than a tree of this sort [. . .] which at this moment (April 28, 1791) is thickly covered with large pendulous branches of yellow, I had almost said golden flowers; for they contain a particular richness, which is impossible to represent in colouring.

~

Right there in the shop where the book lay open on the table, I could see the emerald green of a tūī in flight. I could feel the air vibrate with its beating wings.

~

The garden by the sea is overgrown now. The jasmine has gone wild, its vines arching over the gate, up into the air, searching for something to cling to. The fuchsia is bright and unruly by the fence, next to creamy yellow roses the size of plates. Giant green apples and lemons roll in the grass. A hedge of lavender, once lovingly tended to by my mother, threatens to overtake it all. The kōwhai remains in the back corner, a little spindly and battered by the wind but unchanged, as in my dreams.

~

I read that when the poet and scholar Anna Jackson was looking at the diaries of the writer Katherine Mansfield at Turnbull Library in Wellington, she found a single perfectly preserved kōwhai flower pressed between the pages of one of the notebooks from 1908. 'After all this time, there it still was, still yellow, still between the same two pages Mansfield had placed it between all those years ago. A piece of the world she wrote about was right there as a piece of the world still.'

~

Three young kōwhai have been planted on a low hilltop in Katherine Mansfield Park in Wellington, in the suburb where she was born and where I went to school for seven years. I used to lie under them after school, watching tūī and blackbirds swooping in and out of the trees, yellow tongue-shaped petals spinning in the northerly wind, the grass dampening the backs of my knees and the thick wool skirt of my uniform.

~

In the mid-twentieth century, kōwhai became relatively common English garden shrubs. Semi-evergreen and hardy enough to withstand the cold sea winds of Aotearoa's coastlines, kōwhai thrive in England. They join the many other plants introduced to Britain from its colonies – including tī kōuka (cabbage trees), toe toe, flax and tree ferns, which bend gracefully over brick walls of shaded gardens in the affluent London suburbs of Highgate and Hampstead.

~

When I first saw the yellow tree in London I thought I was hallucinating. It might have been hot enough for that. In the distance, the air shimmered and bent into waves above the asphalt. I walked closer. The tree seemed to be glowing. I felt that if I stood close enough I would be able to see the gold reflected on my skin, like a buttercup held up to the chin. Its slender bell-shaped flowers were full and open, ready to drop at the slightest touch. More than half had already dropped in a pool of yellow petals. I touched them with my foot. I picked up one of the fallen blooms and held it in my hand. I took a picture with my phone and sent it to my mum on WeChat.

~

Heatwaves often occur in fiction as plot devices, forcing characters to contend with the uncomfortable and the unbearable. New York City is often depicted in a heat-wave, as in two of my favourite novels when I was a teenager, *The Great Gatsby* and *The Bell Jar*. The latter famously begins with the particular taste and smell of an inner-city heatwave: 'the hot streets wavered in the sun, the car tops sizzled and glittered, and the dry, cindery dust blew into my eyes and down my throat'. The strange heat of London that day made everything feel luminous, dreamlike, a little unsettling. Would all Aprils from now on be like this one?

~

The tree vibrated in my memory afterwards. I went back the following day, and the next, unsure whether I'd be able to find it again. But it was there, still standing in eerie silence, with no Wellington wind and no noisy tūī to dart around its branches, to sing and suck nectar. Who planted this tree? Did they know where it came from? Had anyone else seen it, stopped in their tracks in front of it, unsure whether they were dreaming? The flowers fell without a sound.

~

My own map of London consists of three lines connecting the places where I've spotted kōwhai trees blooming in and around the city: north, near Bounds Green station; south-east, while driving back to the city from the New Forest (a bright gold blur spotted from the car window); and north-west, on a street just around the corner from my flat. I walked past it one day in mid-autumn. Its frilled evergreen leaves caught my eye. Dried golden petals coated the gravel path. At that time, the news was full of pictures of burning: eucalyptus forest fires in Australia, early scrub fires in Aotearoa. Each year the burning goes on longer and the images grow more surreal. A clip circulating on Twitter showed a charred ridge of flame being whipped into spirals by the wind: a bright funnel of light in mid-air.

~

I attended a poetry workshop where one of the partici-pants asked: 'How do we write about nature without writing an elegy?' I am still trying to work out the answer. I never really intended to write about ecological loss, but I also don't know how to avoid writing about it. I have to begin again, this time with the words of the poet Franny Choi, from her poem titled 'How to Let Go of the World':

in lieu of all I can't do or undo; I hold.
    The faces of the trees in my hands.

~

Katherine Mansfield's short story 'At the Bay', written in 1922, a year before the writer died from tuberculosis at the age of thirty-four, contains what I am sure is a description of a kōwhai tree, though in the text Mansfield names it as a mānuka. But mānuka flowers are neither yellow nor in 'the shape of a bell'. They are white and candy-pink, with rounded petals and pink stamens. Had she mixed up the names? She was living in Europe at the time and hadn't been back to Aotearoa for more than a decade. In the story, set in Wellington, one of the characters gazes up through the leaves while flowers fall around her:

[. . .] if you held one of those flowers on the palm of your hand and looked at it closely, it was an exquisite small thing. Each pale yellow petal shone as if it was the careful work of a loving hand. The tiny tongue in the centre gave it the shape of a bell. And when you turned it over the outside was a deep bronze colour. But as soon as they flowered, they fell and were scattered [. . .] Why, then, flower at all?

~

One unusually warm day in October, the sun touches the back of my neck as I sit on a park bench pulling my socks and shoes on after swimming at the pond. I take out my Thermos, an apple and a book. I'm rereading *Turning* by Jessica J. Lee, her memoir about swimming year-round in the lakes of Berlin. I open the book and out falls a pressed kōwhai flower from between pages 230 and 231. I don't remember placing the flower inside the book, but I think it must have come from the tree in full bloom in Bounds Green, since my copy of this book has never left London. It's like I'm holding a memory or a secret message in my palm, one I myself had left behind and forgotten. I wonder if Anna Jackson felt something similar when she opened Mansfield's notebook in the library. The flower is still yellow, but faded to pale gold just like the colour of the botanical drawing of *Sophora tetraptera* from 1791. Holding it up to the light, I can see the delicate veins that run the length of each petal.

~

Where does spring begin? Where does it end? On the 13th of February I walk around the corner to see if the kōwhai shows any sign of flowering. I notice for the first time that whoever lives here must be a careful gardener: a tender fig tree has been wrapped in gauze to keep it safe from frost. I wonder if they've seen me staring at their tree. I wonder if they were the one to plant it, or whether they inherited it, and if so from whom? The kōwhai's dark evergreen leaves stand out against the bare branches of planes and oaks. I can see bunches of small, pointed buds starting to turn from green to gold.

~

My markers of home are rooted in plants and weather. Wind that tastes of salt, the tūī's bright warbling call, the crunch of shells underfoot, a swaying kōwhai tree. As time passes, these pieces of home begin to feel unstable, shifting further away. Long after I've moved away from Wellington, after my parents moved out of our house by the sea, after the garden has gone wild, a kōwhai tree grows in a garden in London: some small proof that although my pieces of home are scattered, I will always find my way to them.

~

A list of yellow objects: 黄 huáng (*yellow*, also *obscene*, and also the official colour of the Chinese Emperor's court), a racist slur, ripe mangoes at the fruit stall by the train station in summer, egg noodles fried till crispy, winter jasmine, a river that runs from the mountains in western China out to the Bohai Sea, the belly feathers of ring-necked parakeets, dried chrysanthemum buds to be steeped in tea, and the faint wing markings of the kōwhai moth – *Uresiphita maorialis* – whose larvae feed on the tree it's named after.

~

Tidying shelves in the library where I work, I run my finger along the dusty spines of poetry books. A pattern of yellow shapes catches my eye. A small hardback volume, its title embossed on the spine: *Kowhai Gold: An Anthology of Contemporary New Zealand Verse*, edited by Quentin Pope and published in 1930. I stand between the dimly lit stacks holding the book in my hands. Its faded dust jacket is patterned with slender kōwhai blooms all curved in the same direction. There's a fullness to their shapes, as if depicted at their ripest, about to fall. I scan the contents and to my surprise more than half of the poets included in the book are women. Some names I know: Katherine Mansfield, Robin Hyde, Blanche Baughan. Others I've never heard of, including a poet named Dora Wilcox, whose poem serves as the book's epigraph:

And as your Summer slips away in Tears
Spring wakes our Lovely Lady of the Bush
The Kowhai; and she hastes to wrap herself
All in a mantle wrought of living gold.

I try to turn the page and find that they're still folded shut, uncut. This ninety-year-old library book has been leafed through but it has never been closely read. I search online 'how to cut pages of old unread books' and learn that the uncut folds are called *gatherings*, a word I know will stay with me. *A gathering*: a collection, a meeting, and also 'a group of leaves taken together, one inside another, in binding a book' according to the dictionary. The word has a feeling of continuous movement inside it – gather objects and memories into your arms, gather pages together with a needle and thread. I find a scalpel in the book repairs box and slice slowly along the fold, trying to be as neat as possible. The pages fall open.

~

I used to know what *spring* meant; I used to be able to tell where it began, where it ended. When the borders of spring started to shift, my eyes began to play tricks on me, showing me glimpses of yellow in places where it should not be, not yet. I keep seeing yellow flowers all over the city, in brief flashes. On the bus home from work, speeding through Camden, I catch sight of what could be a kōwhai blooming over the balcony of a flat in a concrete block – bright gold, then gone. February is not yet over but the tall kōwhai down the road is already in bloom, two plump clusters of bell-flowers shining at the top. The rest of its buds, which last week were sealed like chrysalises, are opening. I notice for the first time that the character for spring 春, one of the first characters I ever learned, contains a sun 日. In another hemisphere, summer slips away.

~

Plane trees line the River Thames along the promenade where I walk during my lunch hour. In autumn I was asked to write about a memory for a project about the trees along the South Bank. I was assigned a tree: a London plane overhanging the river. But when I went to look at it, I found it hard to see the tree that was right in front of me; instead I saw the rows of plane trees along the streets of Shanghai, planted by French colonisers in the early twentieth century to make the streets resemble Paris. In spring, feathery pollen floated down in the humid air. Did the same thing happen when I saw the kōwhai in London? When I looked at it, could I *really* see it, or was I instead seeing all the kōwhai trees of my childhood? They placed my memory next to the tree, typed on a piece of laminated card. My memory stayed near the tree all day and all night for six weeks. One afternoon I sat on a bench by the river, in view of the plane tree, while tourists strolled along the walkway. Three girls passed by, each with a pink balloon tied to their wrists. In a burst of wind one of the balloons got free, soared up through the branches of the tree, over the pier, into the river's current. The girls clung to the railings and watched it being carried away.

~

In February, pink buds have come early to the plum and cherry trees all over London. Flicking through the March issue of the *The Garden* while waiting for the dentist, I stare wide-eyed at a zoomed-in picture of kōwhai flowers taking up most of the page. This semi-evergreen shrub *Sophora microphylla*, 'Sun King', the columnist says, is plenty hardy enough for English winters – and there's even a smaller variety, *Sophora molloyi*, 'Dragon's Gold', that can be grown in a pot. There's no mention of its Māori name, which to me is its true name. That night I search the Royal Horticultural Society's plant database for nearby stockists of 'Dragon's Gold' – a plant nursery in Hampshire sells young shrubs for sixteen pounds each. I'm nervous, as if I've just decided to adopt some kind of needy pet. I'm worried I'm not ready. Once, I bought a potted kumquat tree and it died seven days later. Last year my dahlias got knocked off my windowsill by the wind and fell two storeys, their heads snapped clean off at the stems.

~

I begin again with the chill of the air-conditioned cinema, where I cried while watching *Frozen 2* during the scene where the forest spirits are able to forgive humankind for all the damage they've done to the natural world. I begin again with the glowing kōwhai, since the tree is where I begin and where I end. I hold parts of the tree in my hands.

~

How do you grow a kōwhai tree? First, gently remove the sapling from its box. Marvel at its smallness. Peel back the fine netting wrapped around its branches. Hold your face close to the leaves: detect scents of mint and lemon. Carry it upstairs in your arms. Feed it, soak its roots to prepare for transplanting. Type into Google 'how to prevent root shock'. Read pages and pages of tips and follow the online advice: 'if you let them get a little root-bound, they seem to flower better the next year'. On your balcony garden, in the rain, tip compost into a larger pot and make a well for the roots to fit into. Begin the tender work of transplanting. Afterwards, check anxiously for symptoms of shock. Position the tree by your front door, next to the climbing jasmine, in partial sunlight. Slowly, day by day, observe its branches starting to thicken, its stem growing more sure of itself. Wait for signs of flowering.

The Language of Waves

Tides

When I got my first period, aged eleven, I had just started in the seventh grade at an American school in Shanghai. It was swimming that I was most afraid of. Not of attracting sharks in shallow waters like boys stupidly said we might, as if they could somehow scare us more than our own bodies already had. I had visions of blood trailing around the swimming pool, not knowing it was coming from me. I had no concept yet of what my body could contain; I thought I might stain everything red in my wake. In English class we watched *The Diary of Anne Frank*, the black-and-white film version. In one scene, there was a small patch of dark blood seeping into the middle of Anne's bedsheets. Some boys looked away.

The sea rises and falls according to the pull of the sun and the moon. When the earth aligns with a new and full moon, daily tidal swells are at their largest. Tides affect the land, too. *Body tides* below the crust of the earth are caused by the same gravitational forces. Near tectonic plate boundaries, these movements may cause volcanic eruptions.

Mene, moon; *mensis*, month; *menarche*, the first period. Much of the folklore and myth surrounding menstruation relates to the cycles of the moon. In Mandarin, one word for menstruation begins with the character for *moon*, which also means *month*: yuèjīng 月经. Across cultures, periods have been associated with magic and supernatural power, as well as danger and uncleanliness. Pliny the Elder famously wrote: 'Hailstorms, they say, whirlwinds, and lightnings even, will be scared away by a woman uncovering her body while her courses are upon her.'

Deepwater

In a small village in Italy, I'm in a gelato shop, in pain and trying to stay upright, when a man I don't know very well makes a racist joke. He's not speaking directly to me but to the group, of which I'm a part. The pain, which had become cool and soft while I sat still licking my ice cream, surges invisibly. There's a wave somewhere deep inside my body.

I look him in the eye and then I have to look away, up at the white pergola covered in plastic vines and pink glistening azaleas. It's difficult to work out what to say, partly because of the wave and partly because the man's small children are present.

It is easiest for me to talk about pain using the language of waves. Deepwater waves are composed of multiple waves of different lengths, formed in deep bodies of water where there are no nearby shorelines to provide resistance. The energy force that propels them is wind.

The pain is the colour of raspberry sorbet, which is the colour of the inside of a person's mouth.

Shallow water

The first time I felt this pain, I was sixteen. I lay on my bed, unable to move except to curl and uncurl my body at regular intervals. I couldn't stop sweating, and the sweat was getting into my eyes. The lilac paint colour of my bedroom walls seemed to be melting off the ceiling and evaporating into faint pinkish clouds.

It lasted no more than two hours, but inside that lilac-coloured mist, time was an unknown thing. The pain dissolved slowly, like lightning strikes getting further and further away. Eventually you can only see the tops of clouds lighting up in the distance, with no sound. Where does pain go when it dies?

It seems counter-intuitive, but tidal waves and tsunami are scientifically categorised as *shallow-water waves*. These types of waves don't need much depth to travel.

Breaking

I am filled with a hot, thick liquid that weighs me down at all times except when swimming. I float on my back and feel a rippling sensation beneath the skin at the base of my spine. I let the blue water hold me. The water cools and cradles me. The water seeps all the way in.

When waves break they break in four distinct ways: by spilling, plunging, surging or collapsing. For three to four days each month, it feels like my body is composed only of these different types of breaking waves. Today I am a combination of plunging and collapsing.

The crest of a collapsing wave does not completely break, but dissolves into white water.

Refracting

The curve of a bay is difficult to discern when you're swimming alongside it, just as the shape of pain is difficult to describe while you're still inside it, unable to see traces of light breaking through the surface.

Some people will ask you for a number, but I find it easiest to represent pain with a colour and corresponding verb. Emerald green gnawing. Crimson pulling. Dark pink pushing.

Refracted waves move in a curved shape where the water close to shore suddenly deepens. Like the thump in your stomach when you take one step further out and there's a drop-off that you can't see: the sand gives way.

Capillary

Capillary waves resemble ripples. They are caused by soft, slow winds blowing near the surface. If you say the word *capillarity* out loud, it sounds like it is composed of sea foam and the white caps of waves.

When the pain slides away, when my appetite returns, I make something hot and soothing: steamed rice, a boiled egg, or instant noodles. I rip open the semi-transparent seasoning packet and tip its contents over the frothing noodles. I watch the specks of dried spring onion, salt and stock powder bubble up and expand on the surface. The steam clears my throat and nose. I warm my hands over the pot and cup steam clouds in my fingers until they disappear. Later, I hold the warm bowl against my stomach.

Internal

When tidal movements and strong winds cause layers of salt water to break apart and combine, the largest waves on earth begin to form beneath the surface.

We first started to find a language for this pain when we were teenagers, when the shame we felt about our periods began to fall away and be replaced by something like anger. We didn't know it at the time, but we were equipping ourselves with a vocabulary for rage. The words we used often related to fire or violence: *My uterus is on fire. My ovaries are trying to kill me.*

Bleeding and pain were brushed over during lectures from the school nurse in Year 7 health class at my Christian all-girls' school in Wellington. We were left with the burning question that hung in the backs of our minds every PE swimming lesson, every pool party: what do you do if you get your period in the pool?

Mentions of periods and period pain are largely absent from the literature of swimming, and nature writing more generally, despite the fact that for many of us, bleeding and swimming are deeply entwined. A few writers have written frankly on the subject. In *Wild*, Cheryl Strayed famously describes inserting her menstrual sponge on the Pacific Crest Trail. In the novel *The Word for Woman Is Wilderness* by Abi Andrews, the main character Erin often experiences period pain while on a journey across the Arctic. 'My womb feels like it is full of acid and lined with tar,' she says. Later, she empties the contents of her Mooncup out onto the ice sheet.

When the hours are punctuated by pain fading and surfacing, my body feels stagnant, heavy. Swimming is often impossible; the walk to the pond is too much. But when I can manage it, floating is a blessing. In *Sanatorium*, a book about floating in water, Abi Palmer writes: 'Floating opens up a world in which I can move with relative ease [. . .] where I can see, think and feel with a clarity I do not experience on land.'

Seiche

I am lucky. For the pain, I get mefenamic acid tablets
from my GP for the standard prescription charge of £8.80.
The little capsules are bright blue on one end, cream on
the other. As far as I know, my pain has always been
believed.

In the poem 'The Institute for Secret Pain' by Kirstie
Millar, a chorus of unnamed women begins to find words
for their collective pain: 'The pain is green and deep and
brilliant.' Another narrative poem, 'The Curse', is a tale
of menarche. A young girl's menstrual pain flares up
during PE class, while swimming: 'There were screams
and a whistle and sunlight streaming onto my face
through the windows above the swimming pool. / And
then there was nothing at all.'

I never attempted to write about pain until I read other
women's accounts of theirs. Before that it was shapeless,
formless. To name it is an attempt to enclose it; to hold
it at a distance and examine it from far away.

Seiche waves, or seiches, are formed in enclosed bodies
of water: lakes, pools, ponds, a bathtub, a cup of
water. Any disturbance occurring at one end of the

body of water – a downpour, an earthquake, a bird – creates pressure and energy that must be released at the other.

Seiche, like a mouthful of warm milk. In the bath, my knees are small islands rising from the ocean floor.

Crushed Little Stars

THE FIRST SONG I ever heard by the American musician Mitski was 'First Love / Late Spring'. I was sitting at my desk in my dorm room in Shanghai. It was the summer of 2016, early June, and I was halfway through my first year of Mandarin language studies at Fudan University. The sky was a pale, polluted blue. My air-conditioning unit was so powerful that condensation formed on the outside of my window. I switched it off and pressed play. I felt the air grow heavy and still in my arms.

I noticed a swelling in my chest and in my stomach, like something about to burst. I noticed how her voice lingered on each word: 'something sweet / A peach tree.'

I'd been scrolling through the album tracklist and was intrigued by the forward slash within the song title. In my own writing, I'd started using the symbol often, both in poems and prose, to signal something essential I didn't fully understand yet, like an attempt to punctuate myself into existing in two places at once. Also, I use it as a way of denoting a line break when setting poetry or lyrics within prose. A breath, a pause, a sharp shift.

/

In the dark cinema, I grew more acutely aware of the distance between his skin and mine. Out of the corner of my eye I could see his face struck by silver light.

He was half Chinese, too, but unlike me, he could speak fluent Mandarin. Unlike me, he talked too much when he felt nervous. Unlike me, he was a man, and as such he was accustomed to taking up space – physical space, conversational space.

At unexpected intervals he offered me small, deliberate touches. A brush of my wrist, a moment-too-long touch of my shoulder. The possibility of this physical contact kept me alert, slow-burning along my spine like a live wire.

I noticed that he spoke with disdain about Asian girls with white boyfriends. 'Those girls wouldn't go near an Asian guy.' When he eventually started to ignore my WeChat messages, I began to entertain the possibility that I was not Chinese enough for him.

66

/

Once, in a stationery shop in Beijing, the woman behind the counter reached out to touch my hair and said, breathless, '混血?' *Mixed blood?*

I was buying a gift for my mum. '你是不是混血?' *Are you mixed?* She smiled, her eyes bright. I nodded at her. I felt pleased to be noticed this way, to be seen. But I wished she had asked before touching my hair.

In China I have always been a foreigner, even though people sometimes recognise that I'm 混血, hùnxuè, *mixed blood*. In China, my hair is the most obviously foreign part of my appearance. It's thick, wavy and a shade of chocolate brown that fades to dark gold in the summertime.

/

I mourned him, but in an adolescent kind of way. Part of me knew I wasn't mourning the loss of a real person but the loss of a fantasy. I went for long walks through the campus at night listening to Mitski's *Puberty 2*. I became more deeply invested in my aloneness. Aloneness, not loneliness.

When I realised that Mitski was part Japanese, I listened again to 'Your Best American Girl' and heard it properly for what felt like the first time. In the song, Mitski, or perhaps a dream-version of Mitski, sings to her all-American boy, her doomed love, 'Your mother wouldn't approve of how my mother raised me / But I do, I think I do.' Her voice starts out strong and whole, then quietens, faltering but intact. At the end of the song, the line repeats but with a different ending: 'But I do, I finally do.'

Many people don't register my otherness straight away, until I reveal it to them. While people of colour can often tell straight away that I'm mixed, white people seem less able to detect any racial difference in me.

/

你的妈妈肯定很漂亮. *Your mother must be very beautiful.*

In the shop in Beijing, I smiled and said nothing. In my head I said, *she is*. My mother has shoulder-length black hair that she has always had curled in a loose perm. I have never seen it straight.

Outside the shop window, snow laced with toxic particles fell from pale clouds.

/

During my eighteen months in Shanghai, I often went to the movies by myself. I could buy movie tickets straight away on WeChat for half the price of tickets back home. I went to see the latest *X-Men* even though I'd never seen a single *X-Men* film in my life. The only thing I remember is Olivia Munn's body taking up the entire frame, her hair long and thick like mine but with streaks of violet. She is a mutant who can shoot lethal rays of purple light out of her palms and she wields a samurai sword.

Munn's mother is Vietnamese Chinese and her father is white American. She spoke both Vietnamese and Chinese until she was five, but drifted away from both languages as a teenager.

After the movie, I cycled home in the dark down the path that cut through campus. There were fallen ginkgo leaves everywhere and giant moths flying at the street lights. Speeding on my bike down the empty street at night was at that time the closest feeling I could find to swimming. With the wind in my hair and light rain beginning to sprinkle my skin, I felt like I was full of purple light, spreading outwards from the middle of my body.

/

In her response to an interview question about the term *half-caste*, the poet Tayi Tibble said: 'When I think of that word, I get an image in my head of being split and split again to the point where you just shimmer like glitter.' Her words remind me of the song that has earned Mitski adoration as a lyricist as well as a performer, in which she sings: 'My body's made of crushed little stars / And I'm not doing anything.'

Some like to talk in terms of fractions: one-quarter, one-eighth, one-sixteenth. I can feel all the pieces of myself getting smaller and smaller. How do I carry them all?

In his essay *Mixed-Race Superman*, Will Harris writes that 'with too many heritages or too few, too white or not white enough, the mixed-race person grows up to see the self as something strange and shifting [. . .] shaped around a lack.' I sometimes wonder if I made myself forget how to speak Chinese. When I was on the cusp of teenagehood, I pretended I didn't have a middle name at all, just a blank space where the word once was.

/

The artist Talia Smith, who is of Pacific Island and New Zealand European descent, documented her experience of returning to the Cook Islands in a series of photos, videos and poem-like texts titled *The heart is the strongest muscle in the body*. One image is of a pastel-pink sunset with blue clouds visible in faint reflections on the surface of a body of water. The sea is a metallic plane of pure colour. On the horizon there's a shape that looks like part of a distant island, but it's not clear. It is the kind of sea I feel I've seen in a dream, completely still and covered in a silvery mist. In the deep blue space between sea and sky there's a thin tear in the photographic paper, splitting the landscape almost in half. Next to the image, Smith writes:

> I wonder if I got my curly hair from my ancestors whose bones are buried on this island.
> [. . .]
> Do bloodlines run that deep and long?

Smith's work is nostalgic and filmic, like watching a string of snapshots from sun-bleached childhood memories with subtitles running underneath. There is an underlying sense of loss, and also tenderness. Remaking memories is an act of tending, of connecting with the past.

I want to make a map of my grandparents' back garden in Kota Kinabalu. I don't know when I will next get to see it. I don't know how much longer it will exist. On my last visit almost a year ago, before Po Po died, there were bedsheets and tea towels hanging from the clothesline: candy-pink and blue gingham, unmoving in the heat. Through them and through the gaps between them I could see vines clinging to the neighbour's metal fence. A green lizard, two dragonflies, a hornet and, in the distance, a white egret standing perfectly still.

Standing by the back door, I remember pointing to a crumbling pile of tree roots. 'Is this where the mango tree was?' I asked Gong Gong, who speaks with me in English. 'Yes, no more of it now. Look, the egret.' We both watched it, smiling. Gong Gong always points out the birds and creatures he can see, wherever we are.

A white egret. Two tall coconut palms, thick vines, a yellow flame tree. I want to lie down in the place where the mango tree stood, where my mum and her younger brother used to gather the hard little fruits and suck their sourness.

/

When I saw Mitski play in London in 2018, a pair of teenage girls stood close to me in the crowd. It was as if Mitski was playing for them and them alone. And in that moment, in their reality, she really was. I watched as they screamed and cried and danced holding each other and I could tell that for them there was only the sound of the guitar chords, her voice, their voices, the pink and gold lights, their bodies, their arms. One of the girls took out her phone at the beginning of each song, not to take pictures but to note down the setlist. I watched while Mitski invented and reinvented punk and indie rock and love and loss for the girls, right before their eyes.

I was experiencing something holy, too. But for me it was different. I feel a sense of intimacy with Mitski's music – I sometimes feel it existing in close proximity to my own work – but I couldn't claim to know or understand her as a person. I deeply admire Mitski, but she's not my idol. Maybe it's because we're close in age or maybe it's because I've read about how realistic she is in terms of her career, about making it sustainable, about surviving long-term as an artist, and I'm trying to do the same.

/

Mitski's band shares the stage with her for all but two songs, but I almost don't notice that they're there. Mitski's movements seem to take up the whole stage, her face serious and serene as if she's in her own world, moving inside her own halo of blue light.

When she begins to play 'Your Best American Girl', a reaction occurs first somewhere in my body, deep at the base of my spine, then in my stomach, then in my hands and wrists, which start to tremble. I try not to cry; I wish my throat didn't feel so tight.

I think of my own writing and how sometimes, making a poem means making something exist outside of my own brain, my own skin. The poem contains parts of me and I still contain parts of it, but it's separate from myself, distinct, new.

/

'Am I even Korean anymore if there's no one left in my life to call and ask which brand of seaweed we used to buy?' Korean American musician and writer Michelle Zauner asks in her essay, 'Crying in H Mart', about the death of her mother and her love of Korean supermarkets. Ever since I first read it, I've been carrying pieces of it inside me. Like Zauner, I'm not fluent in the language of my mother's side of the family. When I was growing up, our language was also one of food. My mother's love is practical, physical. *Are you warm enough? Did you sleep well?* We are clumsy when we try to put our love into words, but we know how to enact it: folding down the edges of curry puffs about to go into the oven, untwisting the purple wrappers from salted dried plums, unpeeling a piece of fruit.

When Po Po passed away, it was too expensive for me to fly to Malaysia for her funeral. I wanted to know what the funeral was like, but I didn't know how to ask my mother the question. Our conversations never normally strayed too close to pain, preferring to sweep aside losses big and small. When I spoke to her via video chat, I tried to imagine myself asking. I imagined the question shooting across the atmosphere over to where she is now, in a different city, on a different continent. I watched the words settle in the air around her, falling in slow motion, in layers of glittering dust.

/

In London, I could feel Mandarin slipping further and further away from me each day, leaving me with scraps and pieces. At unexpected moments the words were on my tongue, ready to spill out of my mouth: 中秋节, *mid-autumn festival*; 经济发展, *economic development*; 华侨, *overseas-born Chinese*. Other times I tried to practise my characters but I couldn't remember how to form the shapes.

I signed up for an evening Mandarin class, my first in almost a year. The morning before the class, I practised writing my name so that when the teacher asked me to write it, I'd be ready. If I don't practise, there are always one or two strokes inside the second character that I forget. 明雅. I split the word in half, then each character in half again: *bright* 明 / *elegant* 雅. A sun 日 next to a moon 月, a tooth 牙 next to a bird 隹.

The Native American poet Layli Long Soldier writes of the burden – and gift – of beginning to teach her young daughter the Lakota language:

> What did I know about being Lakota?
> [. . .] What did I know of our language
> but pieces?
> Would I teach her to be pieces.

/

The way I taught myself how to write my name was by writing it piece by piece. Sun, moon, tooth, bird. Sun, moon, tooth, bird. What is a name? At the sound of your name you stop, you look up, you run, you call back. Your body knows to move towards the sound of your name, even before your brain has fully registered it. In Shanghai, from at least eight in the morning until two in the afternoon most days, I was not Nina but Míngyǎ 明雅. Before then, my middle name had only ever been a middle name, a word I hardly ever heard spoken or said aloud myself. Now my teachers used it all the time, calling it out in class, greeting me with it in the corridors. I began to turn my head towards it. In the sound, I no longer heard just pieces.

At the evening class in an office building in London, no one asked for my Chinese name.

/

The poet Sarah Howe's mother is from Hong Kong, and her father is white. *Loop of Jade* charts her journeys to and from Hong Kong, where she was born. In 'Crossing from Guangdong', she writes:

> Something sets us looking for a place.
> For many minutes every day we lose
> ourselves to somewhere else.

When I first read this poem I was about to leave one home in search of another. If I could, I would ask Mitski where home is, though for me it's a question with an impossible number of answers and for her that may be the case, too. I think of my parents' garden by the sea where the kōwhai grows next to the lemon tree, filling my hands with yellow. I think of a window in Shanghai full of pink light.

/

Physical proof that another home exists: a pair of green lace-up boots, a red scarf, a key ring. These are objects drawn by the artist Jem Yoshioka in her comic *Visits*, where she recounts her first-ever trip to Japan as a teenager. In Japan she 'feels more and less at home than ever', an intensely familiar feeling that reminds me of travelling back and forth between New Zealand, China and Malaysia throughout my life, each time feeling both more and less at home. Back in New Zealand, Yoshioka feels 'a deep feeling of homesickness for somewhere that has never been home'.

The cover of *Visits* is a line drawing of the artist's face and upper body. Her outline is filled in with layers of patterned origami paper in sky blue, forest green, pink and gold. The patterns remind me of a piece of Japanese cloth inside a glass case that I saw at the V&A in London — navy blue silk threaded with a flock of gold-embroidered egrets in mid-flight, wings overlaid with wings.

What do I know but pieces, all at once? In the song 'A Burning Hill', Mitski's voice is expansive, all-consuming:

> I am a forest fire
> And I am the fire and I am the forest
> And I am the witness watching it

Half sun, half moon. Half forest, half fire. A blue lantern, a jade heart, a peach-pink melamine bowl. The shadowy space in me shimmers; I feel its burn and glow. It is a kōwhai forest in a southern hemisphere summer. It is bloodlines, it is threads, it is pieces of cotton hanging up to dry under a coconut palm, sheets of white and pink and blue.

Falling City

1. The apartment building where the writer Eileen Chang lived in Shanghai stands at 195 Changde Lu, at the corner of Nanjing Xi Lu. I found it one day at the beginning of spring, a month after I arrived in the city to study Mandarin. I was obsessed with retracing my steps through the district where I'd lived when I was young, making note of what was different and what was unchanged. I sought out exact places where I had stood ten years earlier. I let bright waves of nostalgia wash over me. I watched them coming from a distance.

2. I knew I needed to stop doing this soon or else something would break.

3. Her Chinese name: 张爱玲 Zhāng Àilíng, given to her by her mother after her English name; *Àilíng* is a direct transliteration of *Eileen*. The two characters 爱玲 mean *love* and *tinkling jade*. I have two pieces of jade given to

me by my mum. They belonged to my great-grandmother, my Gong Gong's stepmother, who was born in Shanghai. One pendant is in the shape of a heart; the other a teardrop. When I clink them together they make a clattering sound.

4. Chang lived in a seven-storey art deco building with curved concrete balconies and dark crimson window frames. The words '常德公园' (Changde Apartments) glow above the entrance, lit up fluorescent gold at night. I must have walked past it a hundred times unknowingly, until one day I passed just close enough to notice a copper plaque by the door.

5. The last time I saw you, it was winter. We were standing on the corner of Nanjing Xi Lu, and I had a clear view of the huge luxury shopping malls on both sides of the street. Things that were different: the crossing had lights, the American diner had been pulled down, yellow and orange marigolds blazed in the middle of the street. Things that were the same: the hotel where my parents and I used to go for dim sum, the plane trees wrapped in purple stars that light up at dusk. I stood in their glow, waiting for the cars to stop.

6. How often she describes the moon in her Shanghai stories: all within a few pages of a novella titled 'The

Golden Cangue', the moon is 'a red gold basin', 'high and full like a white sun', 'that abnormal moon that made one's body hairs stand on end all over'.

7. She is right. Here, the moon is abnormal. I can't remember what it looks like through clear, unpolluted air. Walking back to my room at night, I looked up and the colour of the moon stopped my breath. I tried to take a picture with my phone but it never came out: a pale blur. Everything was in a haze, a sunken dreamworld seen through pink stained glass. It felt like everything around me could have collapsed at the slightest touch. Light, sound, the air that separated you and me.

8. I often recorded observations in my notebook on the flora and fauna of Shanghai, in waking and in dreams: white yúlàn magnolias (the designated official flower of the city) with their dark leathery leaves, plane trees planted by the French, ginkgo trees turning yellow in autumn, plum blossoms, and the azaleas, enormous clouds of magenta and pale pink in courtyards and city gardens.

9. The women in her stories are not always likeable. They are selfish, bored, cruel, petty, trapped in stuffy apartments and unhappy marriages. Shanghai can trap its inhabitants easily, with spring rain that pours unendingly, summer humidity that smothers, drains. One night in

June my electricity ran out at 3 a.m., shutting off my air conditioning. I got out of bed and lay on the tiled floor, damp hair fanned out above my head, fingers spread wide, not touching any part of my body. Every few minutes I shifted onto a cooler part of the floor that my skin had not yet touched. I drifted in and out of sleep. A colloquial word for *humid* is 闷 mèn which can also mean *bored*, *depressed* or *tightly sealed*. The character is made up of a heart 心 inside a door 门.

10. I think of the women in Chang's city, their curled hair frizzing in the heat, a halo of light around their heads. They sit by the window in dark bedrooms and hotel rooms, awake while everyone else is asleep, in silk cheongsam and cotton slippers with peonies embroidered on the toes. City of dimly lit windows and half-open doors. City of smoke moving through still air. City full of trapped hearts.

11. The phrase *New Woman* 新女性 was coined in the 1910s by radical intellectuals who saw the inferior status of Chinese women as a symbol of the nation's outdated traditions. The New Woman of their dreams was well educated, independent, free-spirited. Chang herself may have fallen into this category, but many women she writes about do not. In her novella *Love in a Fallen City*, the protagonist Liusu tells her husband: 'If you were killed, my story would be over. But if I were killed, you'd still have a lot of story left!'

12. A blurred photograph depicts a funeral procession moving down a wide city street. A young woman's portrait held high above the crowd, her face bordered by large chrysanthemums. I can't make out any expressions except for the woman's in the portrait: her head dipped forwards, her eyes cast down, lips painted, studio lights gleaming on her shiny, pinned-back hair. She wears a white dress with a high collar. People stand overlooking the street from the rooftops, their arms waving in the air.

13. Ruan Lingyu was an actress who died from an overdose of sleeping pills on the 8th of March, 1935, aged twenty-four. It was one month after the premiere of the silent film *New Women*, directed by Cai Chusheng, in which Ruan starred as a single mother who dreams of being a writer but is eventually forced into prostitution to support her child. A crowd of 300,000 marched in the streets of Shanghai for her funeral. A caption below the photograph on her Wikipedia page reads: 'The flowers at Ruan's funeral were reported in the press to be as high as the buildings.'

14. When I walk alone through the city at night I am surrounded by this glow, but I'm not sure it's real. I

could reach out and touch you but I'm not sure you are real.

15. What was Chang herself like? I don't know, but I think she understood this moment when the dream and the real begin to blur. She understood how the sky in Shanghai contains many different colours at once: 'At the horizon the morning colours were a layer of green, a layer of yellow, and a layer of red like a watermelon cut open.' Reading her stories in translation is like trying to see her from a great distance. Or through a thick pane of glass. I am standing outside, peering into rooms where her ghost has been.

16. As autumn deepened I expected to see your face on the street or in the subway station. After you left I thought I might feel sad that this possibility could no longer exist. Instead after a while the outlines of trees looked sharper, like a fog had lifted.

17. The Aotearoa poet Robin Hyde was twenty-seven when she visited Shanghai in 1938. She wrote about tasting 'what must be the best chocolate cakes in the world' at a café in the French Concession. I imagine Robin Hyde and Eileen Chang crossing paths un-knowingly sometime in 1938. Browsing in the same bookstore, smoking in a corner of the same dance hall,

crossing the same street somewhere in the International Settlement where Chang lived. Their eyes meet for a moment.

18. In every city, large or small, each person has their own secret map. Reading about the history of Shanghai online, I came across a link: *Map of Haunted Places in Shanghai.* Little red stars mark locations in and around the former French Concession. The Paramount Ballroom, where a young woman was shot and killed on the dance floor in 1941. Chang frequented the Paramount; it was the centre of Shanghai nightlife in the 1930s. The building is still standing. People say they have seen the shadow of a woman in the fourth-floor ballroom, dancing in slow circles by herself.

19. Places you showed me: the tiny ramen bar, the grimy ultraviolet underground club, the Chongqing hotpot restaurant where I waited outside in the rain while you went in to return something your ex-girlfriend had left at your apartment. Afterwards, I couldn't avoid passing by these places, but when I walked past I sped up. Especially at night, when there was a risk of dreams pouring in.

20. In Shanghai, Robin Hyde dreamed of back home: 'Almost every night, lying in the padded quilt, I dreamed about New Zealand, dreams so sharp and vivid that when I woke up, it seemed the black-tiled houses were a fairy-tale.' Back home in Wellington for a few weeks in summer, those first few nights in my childhood bedroom, I dreamed of plane trees, rain-soaked streets, a night sky that was never dark.

21. In the preface to her collection of short stories, *Romances*, Chang wrote: 'Our entire civilisation – with all its magnificence, and its insignificance – will someday belong to the past. If the word I use most often is "desolate" it's because I feel, in the back of my mind, this staggering threat.'

22. It was the middle of winter, and you and I were standing on the corner of Nanjing Xi Lu. From there, I could see the place where she lived, when she was the same age I was then. I walked away when I couldn't stand being near you any longer, knowing that if you touched me again I might burn up in the cold air. I never told you anything important about myself but if you had asked, if you had paused to listen, I would have said: my dreams take place in the rainy season. As I walked away towards the crossing, where marigolds blaze in the middle of the street, my ears were ringing with the chaos of passing traffic, a plane overhead, all of it rolling into the sound of a breaking wave.

23. I can never show anyone my map of Shanghai, not because it's a secret, but because it is so huge and sprawling. The park where there's always an old man playing his saxophone in the pagoda, the pink neon light installation on the side of an abandoned building that I found once somewhere near Huaihai Zhong Lu and never found again, the bookshop café where I used to write – where you can pay ten yuan to send a postcard to your future self. They put it in a box to be posted on your preferred date, which can be months or years or decades from now.

24. 'I'm looking for the first day of spring on the lunar calendar,' says a character named Shijun in Chang's novel *Half a Lifelong Romance*, while alone in a room with the woman he is beginning to fall in love with. Shijun flicks through the calendar on the wall, one of those old Chinese paper calendars like the one on the wall of the dumpling restaurant where I often went for lunch. Weeks' worth of discarded pages lay crumpled on the floor, each printed in jade green ink. I took one, folded it, tucked it in my pocket.

25. A postcard you can get in any souvenir shop: a black-and-white photograph of a young woman with shiny hair pinned back in victory curls. She's a movie star, a pin-up girl on cigarette packets and posters for stockings and perfume and magazines, the girl they called *New Woman*. She is looking directly into my eyes, her lips almost turning into a smirk. I turned the postcard over, looking for her name, but there wasn't one. I sat down at one of the café tables and began to write. It was the first day of spring.

The Plum Rains

CHIHIRO

In the 2001 animated film *Spirited Away*, ten-year-old Chihiro stumbles upon a curved bridge above a dry riverbed. Above her, dark clouds begin to spread over the blue sky, threatening rain. As day turns into night, the real world turns into a strange, luminous fantasy realm. Frightened, Chihiro tries to run back the way she came but finds a vast body of water blocking her path. 'I'm dreaming, I'm dreaming,' she repeats to herself. Her body begins to lose its solid form; she is slowly turning transparent. Half ghost, half girl. The river is visible through her skin.

From this moment on, *Spirited Away* is a film that steadily fills with water: a flooded river, a drenched bathhouse, a train speeding across the sea. Water becomes a boundary between the real world and the spirit world. And as it often does in Hayao Miyazaki's films, rainfall marks a moment of transformation. On her first night working at the spirits' bathhouse, Chihiro is almost fully part of the spirit world. Her clothes have changed from a T-shirt and shorts to a more traditional coral-red tunic, tied at the waist with a red strip of fabric. We see her silhouette through a screen door while red lanterns light up one by one in the pouring rain. Blue hydrangeas shine wetly in the glow of Chihiro's room. She slides open the door into the rain and finds herself face to face with a spirit.

MÉI YǓ

梅雨, méi yǔ, *plum rain*. Late spring to early summer in eastern China is the season of the plum rains, traditionally marking the period when plums ripen and turn yellow. The plum rains are caused by a weather front in the lower troposphere of the sky, where two bodies of air of different densities combine over eastern Asia: the moisture-heavy air over the Pacific Ocean, and cooler air that forms over continental land masses. This causes high humidity and persistent heavy rainfall over eastern China, Japan and Taiwan between April and July every year. In 2020, Shanghai experienced the longest plum rain season on record. The phrase '梅雨' is the title of a poem by Tang poet Du Fu. Many translations of this poem exist, but I decide to look up the original. I attempt my own imperfect translation of the second and third lines: 'the fourth month ripens yellow plums / the clear river flows on.'

For many nights in a row in Shanghai, the rain turned the city luminescent. I was falling into something – not love, but hunger – and my anxiety slipped out of my control. It took hold of my relationship to food and eating in a way it had never done before. One of my Mandarin teacher's favourite example sentences that she used to test our grammar: *eat two meals a day if you want to be beautiful*. The perfect sentence for us to memorise, evenly balanced into two clauses: one imperative, one conditional. The weight of this sentence – and the light cadence with which we repeated it in unison in class – rattled inside my head. I took the words apart one by one.

I got into the habit of listing in my head all the things I'd eaten in a day. So I brought my notebook with me when I went out to eat alone, and wrote down the colours of the sky instead: blood orange, dark violet, strawberry ice cream pink, hot magenta.

It rained all night the first time I went to his apartment. I lay on my side, his spine curving in front of me in the dark as he moved. Briefly I saw between his shoulder blades the outline of a circle in ink, or perhaps two small circles overlapping. I wanted to trace my finger along the deep blue line. He turned onto his back and it was gone. In shadow, the shapes of our bodies were blurred. I suddenly remembered the circles the next day while on the subway home (line ten: the lilac-coloured line with shiny lilac-coloured seats in all the carriages) holding my wet umbrella between my knees where it dripped onto my sandals and the floor of the train. The vision came back the same way a forgotten dream can return hours later, days later, in a brief flash of colour.

Places in the city where reality feels altered: empty subway platforms; the floodlit streets of campus at night; the café with wet plastic vines curled around the doorway where we stood side by side, about to step out into the rain.

SAN

San is first glimpsed through clouds of thick mist and rain, riding on the back of a white wolf, sprinting down the mountainside. At the foot of the mountain, on the banks of a flooded river, Prince Ashitaka and San cross paths for the first time. One of the most iconic stills from the film is when their eyes meet across the river, San's cheeks smeared with the blood of her wounded wolf. In the same moment, a ghostly tree spirit appears.

All of Miyazaki's films have their own vivid landscapes. Most are concerned with imminent environmental destruction of some kind. *Princess Mononoke* (1997) has its own entire ecosystem, made up of emerald-green trees, rivers, mountain valleys, forest sprites, bewitched animals, a glowing lake set deep among the trees. The forest is being cut down and cleared away by humans, and the spirits begin to revolt.

Writer Nina Li Coomes focuses on Miyazaki's heroines as bodies in constant flux, crossing between worlds and between the borders of girlhood and womanhood. Coomes considers these characters through the lens of her own mixed-race heritage. I find myself doing the same. San, a human girl raised by wolves, lives with spirits in the forest and tries to protect them. She is not a wolf, but nor does she see herself as fully human – Coomes asks: 'Is San a wolf? Is she a girl? Is she neither, or both, or something in between?' There is so much shape-shifting; so many doors, bridges and portals that lead Miyazaki's heroines into new dimensions. The borders of the real and unreal are blurred, as are the characters who cross them. I think of Chihiro's arms and hands turning ghostly as she stands by the river, and that first image of San and her wolves emerging out of the mist and rain like apparitions.

Soon after I left Shanghai, after my language course ended, I had a vivid dream: a white temple set into the slopes of a valley, surrounded by lush green forest and fields, a narrow river coursing below. The sky is gleaming blue but darkening with clouds. A pack of white wolves guards the temple. They look up at the sky. A soft rain dampens their faces.

MONSOON

I was sitting in the lounge with Mum and Gong Gong. The wooden clock on the bookcase chimed half past four, and the sky in the window darkened as if something was passing across the sun. Gong Gong stood up to switch on the lights and turn down the humming ceiling fan that blew warm wind onto my skin. There was some kind of cooking programme on TV – a woman teaching her viewers how to make sticky green cakes flavoured with pandan leaves. The lights glowed in the new darkness. Then a cool wind rushing in through the open patio doors signalled the beginning of the downpour: rain hammering the ceiling, shaking the roof and walls of the old house. Gong Gong didn't look up from the TV, but

Mum and I went to the open door. We knew we had minutes until it would be over. Silver torrents of water poured down onto the back garden, drenching the long grasses and the small, shaking mango tree. I was standing in the doorway where raindrops caught my cheeks and arms, where the rain looked like a veil separating me from the garden. I breathed the wet air in. Then the air brightened and everything was quiet except for the TV in the background, flies hitting the windows, rainwater trickling down from the eaves.

Every afternoon is the same during Borneo's rainy season, which falls between October and February. At around four o'clock, the rain comes down hard and fast. This is a different kind of rain to Shanghai's slow, relentless plum rains: these monsoons are sudden, euphoric, surreal.

Borneo's tropical climate means that temperatures stay between roughly 27 and 34 degrees Celsius most days, with little seasonal change apart from rainfall. A 2012 report on the impact of climate change in Borneo noted that based on projections of a 2-degree increase in global temperatures, Borneo will be severely affected by climate change through increased risk of floods, forest fires and sea level rise. This 2-degree increase is a very low estimate; as of December 2019, Climate Action Tracker classifies projected temperature increases of up to 2.8

degrees as 'optimistic'. A projected warming of 4.1–4.8 degrees by the end of 2100 is now considered our absolute 'baseline' trajectory.

It's only possible to romanticise the rain if, like me, you did not grow up in a region prone to flooding. I've visited Kota Kinabalu for years and have often splashed around in this rain, but I have never experienced a flood. Throughout May and June 2020, flash flooding in Kota Kinabalu led over a thousand people to evacuate to relief centres. In her essay 'Everything Anyone Has Ever Said About the Pool', Australian writer Ellena Savage states that low-income women and girls are much more likely to die by drowning in flood regions than men and boys. 'Swimming education is not a neutral thing,' she reminds us.

I'd been visiting Kota Kinabalu during my mid-semester break. My parents joined me there, along with my aunts and uncles and cousins. Life in Shanghai at that time felt too intense, unreal: a fluorescent city made up of longing, hunger, continuous dizzying rain. Back with the joyful chaos of my extended family, we ate together each night. There was always a combination of Cantonese dim sum and Malay favourites on the table: satay, spicy char kuay teow, fried fish, egg tarts, siu mai and bao. All of us crowded round on stools and chairs, the mosquito coils giving off a chemical scent from under the table, and I slowly regained something of my old relationship to food – food as a connective force, a source of strength and joy.

MEI & SATSUKI

At the beginning of the most memorable scene in *My Neighbour Totoro* (1988), a single raindrop causes ripples in a stream, marking the beginning of a storm. As the afternoon darkens, Satsuki and her sister Mei take shelter under a shrine, next to a bush of blue hydrangeas. Later, rain still falling, they wait for their father at the bus stop. In the glow of a street light, the enormous forest spirit Totoro meets Mei and Satsuki for the first time. Raindrops fall noisily from the canopy of ferns, pattering the top of Totoro's umbrella, and he bounces with delight at the sound. The girls stare at the spirit, wide-eyed. Yellow chrysanthemums and irises shine in the dark. The flowers make me think of Chihiro in *Spirited Away*, the way she sprints through fields of dark pink azaleas and purple hydrangeas, their leaves brushing against her shoulders. Like Chihiro's parents in *Spirited Away*, Satsuki and Mei's mother and father are absent for most of the movie. Forest shrines provide brief glimpses of the spirit realm; a world that feels both ancient and strangely close, hidden in plain sight, especially once night has fallen. The friendly spirits lie just beyond a veil of rain, or across a stream, or in the tops of trees. 'It was a dream but it wasn't a dream!' Satsuki chants over and over again in the morning.

DIÀNMŬ

This notebook is A5-sized with a patchy black and white design on the front, similar to those classic American exercise books of the '80s and '90s. It's a thin paperback with shapes and pictures taped to the cover: drawings of constellations, brightly patterned origami paper. The pages are cream-coloured and ruled, with the words *BOSHI PAPER* on the corner of each page.

I still have four notebooks from the year and a half I spent studying in Shanghai. The very first one, which was smaller and had a pale yellow cover, seems to have been lost somewhere between Shanghai, Wellington and London. The black and white notebook, the one closest to falling apart, spans September to December 2016. Inside I've taped boarding passes, a dried ginkgo leaf, a movie ticket, overexposed Instax Polaroids and a ticket for a music festival in Shanghai called 'Concrete & Grass'. There was a thunderstorm on the first night of that festival, which fell on the same night as Mid-Autumn Moon Festival, 中秋节. In my notebook, the next day, I wrote notes on the lightning: we had been watching a K-pop boy band perform their latest Mandarin single when the purple clouds split open with blue light and the stage lights flickered pink and gold. The crowd of mostly teenage girls gasped and screamed every time the lightning came. When the rain started, it drowned out the band – we scattered, running for cover, laughing and reaching for each other in the storm.

The goddess of lightning is Diànmǔ, *lightning mother*. She was born a human girl. Hers is one of few stories I remember learning at Chinese school when I was little, though the details have faded. I can still remember a picture of her from a book of stories: she is tall and lithe, wearing a blue flowing gown, carrying a shining mirror in each hand. One day the god of thunder, Léi Gōng, spies a young girl throwing a bowl of rice into a ditch. He thinks she is wasting valuable food, and consequently strikes her dead. The Jade Emperor, the First God, witnesses Léi Gōng's error – the girl had only been throwing away rice husks, the remains of fresh rice that she had given to her mother. The Jade Emperor brings her back to life and transforms her into a goddess – to be a wife to the god of thunder who had killed her, to light up the sky before the thunder.

PONYO

Ponyo was released by Studio Ghibli in 2008 and was billed as a movie for kids, but in typical Miyazaki fashion, it's punctuated by unsettlingly strange moments. Drawing on Japanese folklore as well as Hans Christian Andersen's story of 'The Little Mermaid', Ponyo is half goldfish, half girl. In her fishlike form, Ponyo befriends a little boy named Sōsuke who lives in a seaside town, and who keeps her in a plastic bucket of seawater. In her attempt to finally become human, Ponyo releases so much volatile magic that she unleashes a tsunami and a typhoon upon the town. What begins as a downpour turns into catastrophic floods. Huge, curling waves take on the form of giant fish as they crash over roads and break against the clifftops. Ponyo runs along the tops of the waves in her red dress, searching for her friend Sōsuke.

But the most interesting character to me in *Ponyo* is Lisa, Sōsuke's mother. She is not just a mother figure; there's a complex background story alluded to in her relationship with Kōichi – Sōsuke's father, who is away at sea – and in her working life as a carer. One of the only trustworthy, caring parents in the Miyazaki canon, where parents don't normally exist at all, she is tough but kind, grumpy but joyful. Her glowing cottage on the hill above the sea is a place of warmth, but also longing, as when Kōichi phones to say he won't be coming home.

After speeding her tiny car up the hill in the wind and the waves unleashed by Ponyo's magic, Lisa bundles Sōsuke and Ponyo in her arms, carrying them towards home. Once safely inside, she flicks on the spare electric torches, spoons honey into mugs of hot water, and puts the kettle on for two bowls of instant ramen. In the dark she opens the curtains and gazes out the windows at the wild sea, unafraid.

We Are All Dreaming
of Swimming Pools

*I think about loving swimming the way you love
somebody. How a kiss happens, gravitational.*

Leanne Shapton, *Swimming Studies*

5, Niagara Falls, Ontario

The orca glides from one end of the deep pool to the
other. Upbeat music plays on the loudspeakers. A pony-
tailed woman wearing a full-body wetsuit stands on a
platform, a white bucket placed by her feet. The music
swells; the crowd leans forward on their seats. I imagine
what it would be like to be in that pool, too, swimming
swiftly alongside the whales under the stadium lights,
perfectly at home in the aquamarine water. My mother
raises her camera.

6, New York City

Half dream, half memory. The bottom and all four sides of the small pool are covered in silvery white tiles. Standing in the shallow end I can feel their ridged edges with my feet. I have my purple plastic goggles with iridescent gold lenses – when I put them on everything is like an underwater sunset. Outside the wide window, a city skyline glistens with heat. After swimming, I eat dinosaur-shaped chicken nuggets and French fries served on a blue picnic plate.

7, Sabah Golf Club, Kota Kinabalu

After our swim, we dry off in the shade next to the pool with our ice creams. Our favourite is the Häagen-Dazs one with chocolate ice cream coated in a milk chocolate shell. Wasps flit around my hair, attracted by the sugar, and Dad swats them away. From up here, we can see dark clouds passing swiftly from above the rainforest towards the town, and I can feel the afternoon heat becoming thicker, sweeter. Mum motions for me to move closer to her under the pool umbrella, getting ready for the downpour.

8, Thorndon, Wellington

Pink nylon, ice-white tiles. An unheated school pool is a lesson in how to breathe. Oak leaves and cracked acorns swirl on the surface of the water as we grope frantically for each other. Chipped fingernails, scraped knees. *One, two! Breathe, kick!* Mrs Ongley's fists are in the air. Anna's nosebleed brings the swimming lesson to a sudden end. Girls gasp and sneer at the little trail of blood droplets on the concrete.

9, Lower Hutt, Wellington

A hazy memory: an indoor swimming pool with high ceilings and a pink water slide spiralling down into the deep end. Every half hour, mechanised waves gently roll the water from one end to another, making our hips sway.

10, Thorndon, Wellington

I dream again of a heated pool filled with deep layers of memory. We huddle by the ladder in our regulation white swim caps and navy swimsuits, a dusting of talcum powder on our collarbones, our arms crossed tightly over our chests. My suit is coming undone at the left shoulder strap even though my mother's sewn it up twice. I grip it self-consciously, worried the last threads will snap. The navy nylon is too small for me now, digging in at the hips. I can't stand having my body out of the water, exposed to the wind, to other girls' stares.

14, Xuhui District, Shanghai

My first two-piece, at fourteen: a black halter top tied behind the neck, with white, blue and pink polka dots, the Roxy logo embroidered on the matching briefs. I take my iPod, a bottle of water, a towel and a pack of Oreos down to the pool next to the car park. All summer, the cool, chlorinated water is a blessing. I float on my back under the corrugated plastic roof, which collapsed last winter under the weight of sudden snow. The lifeguard plays games on his phone while I do my slow strokes, alone. The heat can't touch me: a girl swimming is a body of water.

16, Jinqiao, Shanghai

It's too hot to be outside without some part of your body touching the water. The pool at the compound where my friend Jessie lives is in the shape of a heart, with dark blue tiles on the bottom and creamy white edges. We sit on the side of the pool, our toes dangling in the water, eating mini burritos wrapped in foil that Jessie's mom made for us even though we said we weren't hungry. I chew on the straw of a juice box. The white sun is behind the clouds but still the plastic lounge chairs feel hot to the touch. When boys from the year above us show up on the far side of the pool, we quickly rewrap our burritos and lower our bodies back into the deep end, gliding away.

19, Thorndon, Wellington

After my last exam I catch the bus down the hill. Thorndon pool glistens enticingly in the sunshine, the chemical colour of a blue popsicle. With my purple swimming cap and pink goggles on, I swim slow laps in the afternoon sun for thirty-five minutes. Getting dressed, my long hair feels coarse and a little bleached from the chlorine. It falls in waves around my sunburnt shoulders. My mum tells me to cut it but I won't. I sit on the concrete steps above the pool to eat my bagel, in the exact same spot where I once stood huddled with a group of other twelve-year-old girls, shivering in the wind, trying in vain to cover up our exposed bodies which felt so awkward and new.

22, Karori, Wellington

Inside the aquatic centre it's warm, humid, windowless. I pull on the swimsuit Mum bought me from a department store sale on our last family trip to Malaysia. It's black with a sporty pattern of lilac stripes down the sides. I stuff my thick hair up into my purple swimming cap, sling my goggles around my neck and tiptoe across the yellow changing room floor. I'm terrible at exercising but I've started swimming regularly again in various public pools around the city: Thorndon summer pool, the site of many school swimming sports days of my childhood; Freyberg pool, perched on the edge of the sea; and here at Karori pool, all the way up in the bush-covered hills. When I lift my head above water I can hear the muffled sound of the wind beating against the roof.

I grew up with access to swimming lessons and public swimming pools – privileges that are easy to take for granted when you're a child. The public pool is governed by rigid structures of gender, class, whiteness, the various shapes of our bodies. As Ellena Savage writes, 'In the history of pool rules, there have been, and remain, rules of non-admission, rules of active discrimination. Not to let Aboriginal people in. Not to let female people in. Not to let trans people in. Not to let people in who can't afford to pay.' Inside the doors of the aquatic centre, with its rigid rules that so closely resemble the anxiety-inducing rules of high school PE class, I feel the urge to cover myself up under the gaze of the tall, athletic swimmers with special racing swim caps. Yet I blend in here in this overwhelmingly white space, with my light skin, my brown hair and my ability to pay the entry fee. I breaststroke too steadily for the slow lane, but too slowly for the medium lane. Away from the changing rooms, in the pool itself – a public body of water – I am a stronger version of myself. Sunlight pours through the glass walls around the pool and reflects brightly off my chlorinated skin.

25, Peak District, Derbyshire

A forest pool surrounded by soft ferns and foxgloves bent over by the wind. A blue reservoir glistens through the pine trees on either side of the little pool. The water is cool, soft, the colour of jasmine tea, submerging my skin in flickering red and orange light. This magic place is called *Slippery Stones*, and it's true, the rocks are slick with dark moss. My boyfriend and I are some of the oldest people here – groups of teenagers smoke and listen to Frank Ocean in the grassy meadow, wearily watching all newcomers who lay their towels down, like languid guardians of the pool. I wince as the teenagers cannon-ball one by one into the dark water, aiming for the middle of the pool, the deepest part where you can't touch the bottom. None of them miss. This place feels both wild and safely enclosed, with slow waterfalls at opposite sides of the pool where the amber-coloured water flows out to a steady stream, which in turn becomes the River Derwent.

26, Lucca, Italy

There are wasps in the grass around the path leading up to the pool. A garden pond is covered with netting to stop small children falling in. Pond lilies are beginning to bloom on the surface, blush pink against so much green. I've got my yellow bikini on under my cotton dress, a gingham pattern on seersucker fabric. There are two ripe peaches in my tote bag. I had one for breakfast, too, along with a boiled egg and toast. In August the peaches here are the sweetest, with marigold flesh, tinged red at the core of the fruit. The juice drips down as I eat one after my swim, drying sticky on my thigh.

Unpeel

peeling fruit for someone is a sign
of tenderness, love.

Jane Wong, *Offerings*

I CAN PICTURE my mum's hands most clearly when they
are curled around a piece of fruit. Usually a mandarin,
the thick-skinned variety, with ribbons of orange peel
twirled around her fingers. Sometimes a lychee. She uses
her teeth to crack open the shells. Other times it's a
bite-sized ladyfinger banana, the sort that carries with
it a heavy, honeyed scent. In a single movement she
unpeels the banana and pops it in her mouth whole. I
follow her lead.

Mum collects our peelings and tips them into the blue
compost bin at the bottom of our seaside garden in
Wellington. Throughout the year she spreads the rotted

compost, mixed with soil, at the roots of plants and trees: beneath the lemon tree, the feijoa tree, and the wonky slow-climbing apple tree that produces three or four bulbous, sour fruits each autumn. I pick the apples once their cheeks begin to redden and wash them in the sink. Mum cores and peels them while I roll out the pastry. We toss the pale slices in cinnamon and dark brown sugar.

My best friend at school hated the pithy strands that remained on her small segments of mandarin. Mid-winter mandarins are always the easiest to peel, the tender skin already loosened around the fruit. I became skilled at pulling away the white tendrils, delicately patterned like nerve endings, leaving a smooth unbroken surface. I'd pass the little bean-shaped pieces to her and we would each pop one in our mouths. We'd hold them on our tongues, enjoying the moment before the vesicles burst.

~

In Shanghai, I used to watch the man at the fruit shop peel my giant honey pomelo. In the middle of the long summer break, when campus emptied out and I was almost entirely alone, I was prone to watching strangers' hands. I hadn't touched another human being in months.

The honey pomelo, 柚子 yòuzi, is widely cultivated in China. I'd never seen one before I moved to Shanghai. The character 柚, made up of *tree* 木 and *reason/origin* 由, carries the sensation of something round and heavy hanging from the branches of a tree. Unlike most mandarins and clementines the honey pomelo is not a hybrid, but an original root species of its own: a parent to many other citrus hybrids. (A grapefruit is a cross between an orange and a pomelo.) Citrus fruits, especially mandarins and pomelos, are often left as offerings at ancestors' graves during Qīng Míng, Tomb-Sweeping Festival. People burn joss sticks and eat special candied snacks such as qīngtuán, green balls of glutinous rice flour filled with sweet bean paste. During the Lunar New Year, when they're most abundant, mandarins are symbols of good fortune.

The cutting of a honey pomelo is a violent, tender process. The man at the fruit shop uses both hands to firmly hold the fruit against the wooden board. He takes a long blade and sets it against the pomelo's leathery yellow skin at a vertical angle. He pushes in and it gives way with a soft squeaking sound. The spongy pith is thicker than I realised — almost two centimetres. He pulls the knife downwards, making a long cut from the top of the globe to the base. The same again on the other side. He sets down the knife, grips the edges of the seam, and pulls.

I hear that familiar sucking sound of the fruit's skin ripping away from the membrane. The sound makes me thirsty.

The pieces of shell fall away to the floor. My jewel-pink pomelo is bagged up and handed to me for six yuan. There are empty skins scattered all around the fruit shop's tiled floor like offerings. I carry my naked pomelo home under my arm: my fragrant, sticky bundle. A sugar-sour scent follows me wherever I go. My Mandarin teacher tells me her mother uses the thick rinds for household cleaning. She puts them under the beds and leaves them there to absorb dust.

My first summer as a student in Shanghai was a summer of unpeeling. Almost all others had left campus; I had two months to kill before my few friends would return. I was twenty-two. I had always wanted to return to Shanghai, a city so deeply embedded in my memory, a city I grew to love at a time when I was becoming myself. I'd always promised my mum (and myself) that I would at some point seriously dedicate myself to learning – or relearning – Mandarin. Eager to put off forging a career path with my new Masters in creative writing for as long as possible, I applied for a government scholarship to study Mandarin at a university in China – and got it.

Waves of homesickness rolled over me throughout the summer. Going on dates with strangers made it worse. I had to come to terms with this new way of being, this new aloneness. Swimming, my usual way of reclaiming myself, wasn't an option; the only pools around were inside expensive hotels, and the university pool had closed for the summer. The languid heat and high humidity made time slow down, made moving through the city feel like swimming. I set to work whittling down my daily life to the things I knew might keep me afloat in lieu of daily human contact: I bought a new prepaid Wi-Fi card, enrolled in an online poetry class, illegally downloaded all seven seasons of *Gilmore Girls* and cycled across campus every evening for a bowl of noodles or wontons, and fresh fruit. At the fruit shop that stayed open until late, the table out front was stacked with plastic boxes filled with candy-pink cubes. With a box of cut papaya and a pomelo tucked in the front basket, I cycled back through the violet dusk, warm smoggy wind in my hair.

I'd begun cataloguing the varying pinkness of the Shanghai sky with my phone. On days when my VPN app let me through, I posted square pictures of magenta clouds on Instagram and Facebook, watching the tiny red hearts of other people's likes popping up from all the different time zones where my friends lived: mostly

Aotearoa, but also Europe, Canada, America. I didn't speak to anyone face to face for almost two months, while my phone buzzed and lit up with messages from far away.

Towards the end of summer I responded to a WeChat job posting from a Shanghainese mother looking for an English tutor for her daughter. I took two subway trains across the city to meet with her at a McDonald's, where she bought me a raspberry-flavoured ice slushy and admired my tattoo. Her daughter was shy, though she liked telling me in careful English about her favourite manga comics. I took the job, and at their kitchen table every week their Scottish Fold cat sat wide-eyed on the table between us, purring at me. I'd stay for dinner, and both mother and daughter together taught me how to use my fingers, knuckles, teeth and tongue to unpeel and eat tiny Shanghai freshwater crayfish, 小龙虾 xiǎo lóngxiā, *little dragon shrimp*. It was a labour-intensive process of picking, peeling and sucking sweet flesh out of each crimson shell.

The long, achingly hot summer faded out with the promise of a trip to the picturesque southern city of Guilin with three of my classmates: Katrin, from Frankfurt, and Adi and Frances, also from Aotearoa. On the sixteen-hour overnight train – far cheaper than the bullet train – the others played cards while I kept watch for the snack cart, which was piled high with vacuum-packed dried sausages, preserved eggs, fresh fruit and endless styrofoam cups of instant noodles. The two characters of Guilin, 桂林, together mean *sweet osmanthus forest*. In early autumn, the region lives up to its name: all the roads are coated in delicate white-and-yellow flowers. Guilin's dramatic karst hills, and the Li River that curves between them, are depicted on the back of the Chinese twenty-yuan note. I had been to Guilin before, almost a decade earlier, on a school trip in eighth grade. I remember sitting with two of my best friends on the edge of a curved stone bridge, our feet dangling over the edge, watching dragonflies and drinking mango smoothies. At night the market streets were lined with fairy lights. The limestone hills fell away in darkness, then reappeared at sunrise like giants guarding the town, silhouetted against the blue dawn.

The others wanted to climb one of the smaller limestone mountains, Lao Zhai Shan. I reluctantly agreed, knowing I'd be trailing along behind them. After half an hour up the winding track my body was aching. I focused my senses on my surroundings in order to keep placing one foot in front of the other. In the shade of the bamboo forest we were kept cool from the strong sun, and through the gaps in the trees I could see graves and burial mounds set into the hillside, much like the hillside cemeteries in

Kota Kinabalu. I could see that the concrete graves had once been painted in pastel colours, peachy pink and baby blue, now faded. Bowls of oranges and chains of plastic white and yellow chrysanthemums had been left as offerings. I relaxed into the soft silence punctuated by our deep breathing and rustling leaves, a particular blending of sounds I hadn't heard since being back home, walking the bush track up the hill above the sea.

After an hour, the canopy of leaves began to clear. The sun warmed my face. The last section of the climb was too steep for any proper path. Instead, a series of rope and steel ladders were hammered into the side of the rock. I shut my eyes and followed my friends, not looking down but only straight in front of me, at the pale, scratched limestone rock.

At the summit, out of breath, I turned to see the view. The Li River in miniature, a luminescent blue ribbon curving between jagged limestone slopes that seemed to go on forever. Between the mountains, smaller valleys had been carved into terraced rice fields. A buzz of insects filled the air along with our breathless laughter: yellow and blue-winged butterflies flitted between us, and giant wasps. I cut a peach into quarters for the four of us and Katrin presented a plastic bag filled with mandarins, bought from a streetside seller at the foot of Lao Zhai

Shan. We peeled and feasted under the small wooden pagoda, letting the juice run down our wrists.

~

At home we use one single word to mean *skin*, *rind* and *peel*: 皮 pí, five strokes. It's a word I've become so used to that it's the one I reach for in certain contexts. *Dumpling skin* and *dumpling wrapper* don't quite cut it, whereas pí touches on exactly what I mean to say, something halfway between the texture of skin and the practicality of wrappings. Sometimes, I only want to eat the skin. When I was little, I was so picky that I didn't want to eat the inside of har gow – I would pierce a hole with my chopstick in the shiny steamed dumpling and squeeze out the pink ball of shrimp, leaving it in the bottom of my rice bowl, and then I would chew on the silky har gow pí.

I read an article in *The Straits Times* about eleven different types of mandarins, and I realise I've been eating them all my life without knowing their names, which are like musical notes: ponkan, lukan, kinno, mikan, mandelo, dekopon.

Later, after I'd moved to London, my mother accepted a new job in Beijing. My parents packed up our house by the sea and set off in August. For them, the end of a Wellington winter turned into a Beijing autumn. I felt a new and acute sense of loss: a definitive end to a part of my life I'd been holding on to still. I saw the garden, the sad apple tree, the kōwhai and the giant red aloe that shields the house from sea salt and wind. The bedroom I painted purple when I was sixteen; the kitchen where we stacked cold oranges in a bowl by the window.

I visited Beijing in deep winter. At the breakfast table at my parents' apartment, we sat in silence as my mum peeled a giant mandarin onto a paper napkin and passed me the segments. The vesicles were so big I could feel them bursting one by one on my tongue. This is a type of mandarin I've never seen in Aotearoa. Cultivated in Korea and Japan, it's known as *hallabong* in Korean and *dekopon* in Japanese. It has two names in Mandarin: 不知火, which literally translates to *unknowing of fire*; and 丑橘, *ugly orange*, because of its strange shape. It is the size of a large apple with an unsightly little bump upon its crown. After the fruits are harvested in mid-winter, the ugly oranges are left for a month to let their sugar content soar, making them honey-sweet and lightly acidic, like raspberry lemonade.

I study each of the characters, trying to unpuzzle them. The names circle in my head like nursery rhymes. 不知火, bright fiery fruit; 丑橘, ugly fruit of deep winter. The best oranges grow in the coldest winters.

The name '不知火' is derived from another Japanese word for the fruit, *shiranui*, which is also the name of a type of atmospheric *ghost light* in Japanese folklore, seen at certain times of the year near the island of Kyushu. Shiranui is said to take the form of pale red lines of light, or sometimes a flickering ball of light, appearing in the sky above the sea at low tide just before dawn.

I first tried one of these oranges three years ago. My first winter as a student in Shanghai was coming to an end, and so were the waves of homesickness that would pull me under without warning. In mid-March, the giant knobbly fruits appeared in large quantities at the fruit stand outside the campus gates. Each orange was individually wrapped in its own paper bag stamped with red Chinese characters that formed a border around the edge. They were three times as expensive as the baby mandarins I ate by the handful, which had kept me going through the wet winter. I bought just two to begin with – four yuan each. I peeled and ate one on the street under my umbrella. February had been the month of baby mandarins. March would be the month of ugly oranges.

~

When I think of home, I see a lemon tree. The yellow fruits are beginning to bulge and fall. Throughout winter and spring, the house smells of citrus rinds. Here, nothing goes to waste. Mum collects mandarin peels and cut lemon skins and places them in a dish in the oven after cooking, so that as the oven cools, it gives off a bittersweet, hot-sugar scent. The rinds begin to dry out and curl in the warmth while the dog sleeps at our feet. Not far away, we can hear waves roaring in a southerly gale. Our skin smells of salt and oranges.

Faraway Love

*Is there really a London? and are you in it? or am I
thinking of, and writing to, a wraith?*

Vita Sackville-West in a letter to
Virginia Woolf, 4 February 1926

Falling Blue

The city is dark when I arrive and dark in the morning
when I wake. Everything is grey, soft pieces of transparent
blue coursing down the sky like sheets of cellophane. I
am still caught in the haze of travel and my eyes can
only focus on one thing at a time; the bare tree branches,
frozen leaves coated in powdered sugar-frost, ice-crusted
mud. Back home, the hills surrounding the harbour are
always green except in September, when the kōwhai and
gorse flowers bloom yellow at the same time. I'm not used
to this much grey. London is not somewhere I thought

I'd end up; I moved to be in the same place as the person I love, and other than them, I know no one here. To fight the lack of colour, I buy pink claw-hearted tulips from the flower market, ones that were grown somewhere far away. At the Vietnamese grocer on Kingsland Road, I buy a little kumquat tree and place it by the window. Within a few days the edges of its leaves begin to curl.

This Rain

I do not see her at first. I walk right past her in the gallery towards other corridors and other rooms. On my way out, my bones are slower, heavier, and she is still there. I glance at the painting without seeing anything at all: an empty canvas of pale rectangles. I take note of her name in my mind – Agnes Martin.

It is my fourth day in the city. The darkness is interrupted occasionally by bright white lines at certain times of day. A pulsing warmth comes from them that I cannot touch. I watch each morning but they don't always come. It is surreal to be here, suddenly in the middle of winter. I spend my days wandering the neighbourhood and searching for jobs online. Once before in my life it had been necessary to teach myself how to be alone in an unfamiliar city. I begin to feel now, acutely, that this is another one of those times. I go out into the cold, I cover my face, I cover my eyes.

Rain Study

I send out several job applications each day. I write the same thing again and again – 'thank you for taking the time to consider my application'. I have never felt so far from the sea. I put on my coat and scarf and walk to the churchyard, where hyacinths and daffodils raise their bright faces above a layer of snow. On the iciest day, I take cover again inside the white halls of the Tate. Again I pass the white painting by Agnes Martin, which I notice is titled *Faraway Love*. The words make me pause and look closer. At first glance, the artwork looks like nothing but a bright square of white. No one is looking at it – instead, everyone is walking past towards the flaming orange Rothko at the end of the corridor.

Stepping closer, I can see that it's covered in faint gridlines that look like they've been traced in sharp pencil. I step away again and it's as if the surface of the painting has changed, like a shock wave has rippled through it, and it has rearranged itself back into its original composition. The pale squares offer light and warmth. On another day, in another season, perhaps they'll give off a different element: wind, rain. The more I look at it, the more it looks like the bottom of the deep end of the swimming pool surrounded by concrete that's too hot to walk on with bare feet. I shut my eyes and lower myself in.

Morning

I am the best at being alone when cooking and eating a soft-boiled egg. Each of us has inherited a different way of timing the boiling of an egg, like cooking rice.

In this blue kitchen I still don't know my way around, I repeat the same set of steps each morning. I fill the smallest pot with tap water and set it on the stove. I take a cold white egg from the fridge, close my fingers around it, slip it in. I watch for tiny bubbles forming on the surface of the shell. When the egg begins to tremble, I get the toast on. When the toast pops, the egg is done. I lift it out with a teaspoon and tip it in an egg cup, like my mother used to do for me, except that this egg cup is not mine. This egg cup is made of cream-coloured china covered in a blue chequered pattern, with a red line around the rim. I tap twice on the egg with the back of my spoon to crack the top, then scoop it clean off. I dip the tip of the spoon inside to break the membrane of the hot yolk. Outside the window, blue dissolves into skimmed milk. A writer friend once asked me: 'What are your rituals?' I wasn't sure then, but now I know.

Untitled (Study for 'The Egg')

There are many other women who cook and eat their boiled eggs alone, like I do. In an early short story by Katherine Mansfield, 'The Tiredness of Rosabel', Rosabel's simple meal of a scone and a boiled egg becomes a kind of symbol of her aloneness in London. In *The Handmaid's Tale*, the narrator has a boiled egg in her white room each morning:

> The shell of the egg is smooth but also grained; small pebbles of calcium are defined by the sunlight, like craters on the moon [. . .] The egg is glowing now, as if it had an energy of its own. To look at the egg gives me intense pleasure.

Apart from her body, the egg is the only other object in the room. She imagines placing the warm egg between her breasts. The egg is a lunar landscape; an empty desert; it is the moon illuminated by the sun. Its shape is the shape of her body: earlier in the text she describes her form as 'a cloud, congealed around a central object, the shape of a pear, which is hard and more real than I am and glows red within its translucent wrapping'.

In a poem by Kim Seon-U, 'Time for Boiling Eggs' (translated into English by Emily Jungmin Yoon), the speaker cooks a boiled egg for her mother, who no longer recognises her:

> (Mom likes them soft-boiled) Fill the pot with water, place the eggs in, and turn on the gas Inside the pure chewy whites, the yolk, a universe that was about to become life (We eat, feed, and are eaten)

The Egg and *Untitled (Study for 'The Egg')* are two drawings by Agnes Martin that examine the symmetry of the egg. They are small compared to her paintings, about the size of an A4 sheet of paper. In *The Egg*, an oval shape is composed entirely of fine horizontal lines that begin to disappear and blur into each other when you look at the drawing from far away. There are subtle variations in the weight of each line, creating a gentle illusion of movement, as if the egg was slowly spinning on its axis. For *Untitled*, Martin places the egg over a grid, cutting it in half lengthways. Then she cuts a line across the top, exactly where you would slice the top off with a spoon.

With My Back to the World

Agnes Martin left New York City in 1967, when she was fifty-five, and went to live alone in the desert. She lived alone all her life, though she had several relationships with women. She suffered aural hallucinations due to schizophrenia, and underwent electroconvulsive therapy for it.

In New Mexico she built herself a studio out of brick and earth. The soft-hued paintings of her years spent surrounded by this landscape and nothing else are defined by bands of colour overlaid with faint grids and lines, surreal in their geometric perfection, but also like a dream that takes place in the desert. *Faraway Love*, the first painting of hers that I saw, was painted in 1999, when she was eighty-seven. As with poems, my responses to artworks are instinctive and come from somewhere inside my body. I can only write about art in terms of intimacy, or a lack of it. In the gallery, I took notes from the little squares of text next to each painting and I sketched the lines that separated her fields of peach and fields of blue. As the London winter brightened into spring, I began to write again.

Martin is very soft-spoken in a recorded interview from 1989, of which a five-minute excerpt can be listened to on the Archives of American Art website. A loud static fills the spaces between her words. The static is made up of soft blue and grey wavering lines that never touch.

On a Clear Day

It is possible to become intimate with a city by eating out alone in the winter. I order rice noodles with roast duck on the second floor of a restaurant in Chinatown, where the only other person alone is an off-duty chef counting his cigarettes onto the table. *Siu ngo laai fan*, a Cantonese phrase Mum taught me how to say once while we waited in an airport food court, though I could never get all the tones right. Later, on the top floor of Foyles on Charing Cross Road where everyone else also looks like an unemployed writer newly arrived in London, I spread cold clotted cream and raspberry jam on my over-priced scone.

In the Vietnamese restaurants on Kingsland Road in east London, we – all of us women in our twenties and thirties, all of us slurping phở in the middle of the day – warm our cheeks in the steam that rises from our bowls and coats the windows, shielding us from the gaze of passers-by. We don't speak to each other, or to anyone else. We wrap scarves around our faces and step out into the melting snow.

Tender Gardens

Seventh Lunar Month

小暑 *light summer ~ season of scorched hydrangeas*

'The Chinese were in fact very friendly, very nice to each other. Not what you'd expect.'

In the white-gold kitchen, the lights above the table are glinting. Pink and purple sweet peas in a vase on the table flutter in a breeze coming in from the open window. I feel my friend's body become tense next to mine. I look out the window, because I can't look at him or anyone else. The heads of blue hydrangeas are swelling and pulsing in the manicured garden. Lily pads tremble on the surface of the hot, brown pond. Dusk is beginning to fall.

I am staying with a close friend and his parents in southern England during the summer. Over breakfast, I had asked his mother about the flowers in her garden: hydrangea, peony, azalea, nasturtium. There are flowers I recognise but don't know the names of; she points to each one and tells me their names, giving me the vocabulary to write about plants with precision for the first time. *Azalea, clematis, dahlia, allium.* I recognise that in doing so she is giving me a gift. She notices trees and flowers wherever she goes; she knows all their names. Two years ago, in spring, she visited Hong Kong – her first time in Asia. Hong Kong was so much greener than expected. 'So much green.'

Her words were partly meant with good intentions, but I don't know how to carry them within my body. Possible responses circle around my head and I can't sort through them all. Would she think of my mother as *a Chinese*? Does she think of me as half *a Chinese*? If yes, how did she think I would respond? If not, then what am I to her? Instead of asking these questions, I say nothing.

Afterwards, in the car on the drive back to London, my friend pulls over beside a red letterbox – one of many features of the English landscape that seems toy-like, unreal – and presses his forehead against the steering wheel.

When I was last at my own parents' house, I read a book of theirs called *A Field Guide to the Birds of China*. On page 18, the beginning of a chapter titled 'The Avian Year', the rhythms of certain lines leapt out at me:

China lies north of the equator
And in the long days of the northern summer
The birds are migrants descending in winter

According to the ancient Chinese lunisolar calendar, which is an agricultural calendar, each lunar month can be divided into two jiéqi 节气 – *solar terms*. Each solar term can be divided into three micro-seasons. These micro-seasons mark a single event in the life cycle of plants and animals. This means there are seventy-two small seasons within one lunar year. Every five days brings a new season.

When I first learned about the seventy-two seasons, I obsessively translated and wrote down the most poetic ones I could find. I discovered that I was born during *the month of lined clothing*, in *the solar term of summer's arrival*, in *the season of the untangling of deer antlers*. My mum was born during *the season of wild geese flying north*.

Twelfth Lunar Month

夏至 *southern summer solstice ~ season of pōhutukawa flowers*

'If you spend too much time in China, you might end up looking like this.' The woman places one finger at the outer corner of each of her eyes and pulls. She laughs. She's not addressing me, but the people standing next to me. Cold breath leaves my body. I feel the urge to run to my dog, Toby, who is waiting for us in the back of the car, to hold his soft ears and press him close to my face. I resist this urge.

David and I are back in Aotearoa for Christmas after a year in London. We've just come in from a walk on the beach and my dry lips taste like salt. The skin around my ankles is rough with sand and the hem of my dress is wet, heavy. We are almost within swimming distance of the great island that guards the shore, Kāpiti. Once the settlement of the Māori chief Te Rauparaha, then a whaling station, now a protected bird sanctuary, Kāpiti lies off the coast of the lower North Island. I've known it since I was small; on our weekends spent on Waikanae Beach, the island loomed over me. Dad always told me that in the ridged shape of the island you could see the silhouette of a sleeping man. With one eye shut, I used to stand on the beach and trace the outline of its shape with my finger. The island is a witness to what has occurred, is still occurring. The island is my witness.

It's January, midsummer up on the coast. In the northern hemisphere it's midwinter, *the season of wild geese flying north*. It hasn't rained in two weeks and the edges of roses are beginning to scorch. Back in London, before we left for the holidays, I planted spring bulbs (daffodil, iris, hyacinth) in plastic containers and placed them in a line along the windowsill. I sent pictures of my not-yet-blooms to Mum, who replied to say she couldn't wait to grow some water hyacinths for the coming Chinese New Year.

Twelfth Lunar Month

冬至 *deep winter ~ season of bulbs in the snow*

Is my otherness becoming more or less visible? Sometimes more – other mixed-race women and women of colour occasionally approach me at work, kindly curious, wanting to know. 'You're mixed, aren't you?' they ask gently. Sometimes less – in a room full of white people they count me as one of their own, turning me into an invisible witness to their casual racism.

I began to realise the importance of keeping a record. I couldn't carry all the details in my body any longer. I needed somewhere to put them down, so I opened a new Google Doc and gave it the title *'INVISIBLE DOCUMENT'*, as if a spell of invisibility might help to lessen the weight of it. The pages were full of incoherent notes, sensations and images collected in the hours and days after something like this happened – an offhand comment from a family friend, racist jokes overheard on a train. I have never been a victim of racist violence or direct harassment; the things I was recording didn't feel important in the wider picture of systemic racism and colonialism that my birth country of Aotearoa, and my adopted country of England, are founded upon. But I knew I should record them. I knew the words themselves were another form of violence, casual and sprinkled with laughter, traded between white people who roam exclusively in white spaces – in the form of in-jokes, teasing and outdated slang that serve no purpose other than to alienate and to control: *coloured, Oriental*.

It was around this time that I also started to keep a garden diary. I tried to imagine a garden of my own, here in London. On my small balcony, I began with three cardinal seasonings of Chinese cooking: garlic, ginger and spring onions. Later, I chose fragrant plants and shrubs that reminded me of home: rosemary, lavender, jasmine, the kōwhai tree. Like the writer Alexander Chee with his rose garden in Brooklyn – 'The first sunlight hitting my windows at seven-thirty and touching the ground in the back around eight' – I studied the movement of sunlight across my north-facing garden. I began to learn by heart the shifting patterns of light and shade. Now I had two diaries at the same time: one full of difficult words, gaps and silences; one full of nourishment, roots, sun and rain.

2/5/18
As soon as the days started getting longer,
our back deck has transformed. I've been
tracking sunlight: warm morning light from
about six thirty a.m. until ten, then again in
the afternoon, from about four o'clock until
about seven. Whereas in winter it's dark,
damp, cold, coated in moss.

I keep finding forgotten flowers inside forgotten books.
I found a purple crocus pressed between the pages of
my copy of *A Cruelty Special to Our Species* by the
Korean Canadian poet Emily Jungmin Yoon. Crocuses
bloom in late winter through to early spring, so I must
have picked the flower then, and put it in the book for
safekeeping. Its petals have turned translucent,
rendering the poem 'Bell Theory' visible *through* the
flower itself:

How to say *azalea*. How to say *forsythia*.
Say instead golden bells. Say *I'm in ESL*. In
    French class
a boy whose last name is Kring called me *belle*.
Called me by my Korean name, pronouncing it
    wrong.
Called it loudly, called attention to my alien.

140

The speaker of the poem begins accumulating half rhymes, small chiming bells: *lie*, *lie*, *library*, *azalea*, *library*. I'm reminded of a line from another poem by Rachael Allen: 'Women's bodies collect materials the way metals accrue in organs.' I begin collecting the names of flora that sways in the background of my memories: azalea, magnolia, hydrangea, jasmine.

I am split between northern and summer hemispheres, and so my own seventy-two seasons are different. I observe my little garden passing through the micro-seasons. *Season of sunflower seedlings, season of wet jasmine, season of cabbage butterflies alighting on brassica leaves.* But what does it mean to attempt to put roots down in a country that forever finds you alien, an outsider, exotically mixed?

Lunar New Year

立春 *the beginning of spring ~ season of glasshouse orchids*

'On which side, your mother or your father?' He asks the question aggressively, without preamble. The man, a friend of a friend, stands in the doorway of my blue kitchen, his body taking up the entire frame. He leans over me and I can see pores in the damp skin of his nose. He smiles down at me in a way that looks like he's baring his teeth.

Behind me, steam rises from the pot of boiling water where the jiǎozi I made for our New Year dinner are cooking. When they begin to rise to the surface, it means they're ready. It's one of those cooking techniques I can't remember learning, one my mum must have taught me at some point, just like she taught me how to put my forefinger in the pot of uncooked rice and pour cold water up to the second knuckle. I turn away from him to lift them quickly from the pot and answer quietly, 'on my mum's side'. Steam coats the walls and my skin.

In late February, David takes me to go see the orchids at Kew. Every winter Kew Gardens holds its annual orchid festival in the glasshouses; each year a different tropical country is chosen as the theme. This year it's Thailand. Up close, the orchids look more like animals than flowers. Pink mouths, violet tendrils, yellow tongues pressed up against the steamed glass. Their ancestors once grew wild in the rainforests of Southeast Asia. There are curtains of climbing fluorescent blooms above a koi pond and a floating fibreglass Buddha surrounded by tea candles. I'm not sure if the display is meant to remind me of home, or if it's specifically designed to make English people feel like they've stepped into an exotic jungle. It can't quite be both.

When we exit the make-believe rainforest and re-enter wintry daylight, I see that the lake by the glasshouse is frozen. The fountain is encrusted in ice. In the gift shop I buy a dark purple orchid for £4 from the sale table, even though I know that means it's probably half dead.

9:57 PM
do you have any orchid care tips?
what should I do once the flowers are
drooping?

Mum 10:40 PM
Prob means they are ready to drop!
Main thing is to resist repotting them.
Only a little water. Do not put in direct
sunlight – too hot; avoid windowsills.
But still lots of light.

First Lunar Month

雨水 *rainwater ~ season of cold mandarins*

Who was the first New Zealand Chinese woman writer? If one like me existed prior to the mid-twentieth century, their name has not been remembered. 'We had no artistic or literary role models,' poet and novelist Alison Wong writes in her essay 'Pure Brightness'. Chinese immigrants first arrived in Aotearoa in the 1850s from war-torn southern China, settling in the gold fields of Otago. It was uncommon for wives to immigrate alongside their husbands, and as a result the earliest Chinese communities in Aotearoa were almost entirely male. Following growing anti-Chinese prejudice from organisations such as the Anti-Chinese League and the White New Zealand League, in 1881 the government passed the Chinese Immigration Act, introducing a £10 'poll tax' on the head of every Chinese person wishing to enter the country. In 1896, the poll tax was increased to £100. It was not until 1934 that this was lifted, allowing Chinese to settle as refugees fleeing the Sino-Japanese War. In 2002, the New

Zealand government offered a formal apology to the Chinese community for the harm caused by the Chinese Immigration Act.

Wong describes the sinking of the SS *Ventnor* off the coast of Hokianga in 1902, a ship carrying the exhumed bones of 499 Chinese people to be brought back to China for reburial in their ancestral villages. Chinese associations regularly organised for remains to be sent back to China for burial; or for those buried in Aotearoa who had no descendants there, they took on annual Tomb-Sweeping Festival customs to honour the dead. Wong recounts a gathering that took place in April 2013 on the beach in Hokianga to commemorate the tragedy:

> We bow three times before apples, mandarins, almond biscuits, roast pork, baak jaam gai with feet and legs and head, red paper folded in the beak. We scatter rice tea wine; burn paper money gold; eat pork and baak jaam gai, an unwrapped sweet on the tongue. Electric fire crackers bang bang bang over the sand.

How many hungry ghosts can the sea hold? Like Alison Wong, long-ago sea voyages are a part of my ancestry. From England to Aotearoa on one side; from the Hakka regions of southern China to Malaysia to Aotearoa on the other. When I ask Mum what we know about Po Po's early life, I get a series of tentative facts. She was (*likely*) born near Hong Kong and fled war as a young girl with her family by boat to the Malayan Peninsula. Her father, my great-grandfather, (*probably*) didn't make the boat or (*possibly*) died on the journey.

Wong's poem 'The River Bears Our Name' contains two places that are in my bones. It is the first time I have encountered my two homes together in a single poem. I can feel it unfurling somewhere deep inside me, as if it has always been there.

> As the sun eases red over Pauatahanui
> You stand alone at the Huangpu River
> Layers of dust catch in our throat
> The water is brown with years of misuse
>
> You stand alone at the Huangpu River
> Your card lies still open on the table beside me
> The water is brown with years of misuse
> I write out your name stroke upon stroke

In moments of grief we offer up flowers, fruit, poems. Whenever we drove from the airport round the coast of Kota Kinabalu to my grandparents' house in Likas Bay, we would pass the great blue mosque and the Chinese cemeteries up in the hills, their colourful gravestones cascading down the hillside. On the graves nearest the side of the road, I could see plastic flowers and wisps of smoke rising from burning joss.

After she died, Mum cleared out Po Po's kitchen. When we next saw each other, months later, she gave me a box of her kitchen things: ivory chopsticks with the words '百年好合' engraved on the handles, floral-patterned melamine trays we had picked for her at Daiso, enamel mixing bowls and an indigo blue pot with a matching lid. I select the blue pot as a new home for my orchid from Kew Gardens.

Second Lunar Month

惊蛰 *the awakening of insects ~ season of*
first magnolias

'Lots of the Chinese students at my school seem to be
scared of dogs.'

'That's because they eat them.'

When the man seated across from me says this, a
white-hot cloud of light billows up from the centre of
the room, or from the centre of me. In the split second
after his words settle on my skin, I could choose to
breathe or not breathe. I could speak or not speak. The
plate on my lap holding a warm chocolate brownie tips
forward. Melted vanilla ice cream dribbles over onto the
dark blue fabric of my skirt.

'That was racist,' I say into the air, into the circle. My
voice is calm. For a moment my voice is present among
the others' voices, and then it isn't anymore. If anyone

else in the room has heard me, they don't make a sign. The room cannot hold on to my words for too long or else it might go up in flames. The room cannot hold on to me.

Over the course of the following day I feel sick and shaky. I have no appetite, except for wanting to chew on something rich and soft, like a Cadbury caramel egg. Unable to sleep, I get up in the middle of the night and cut a blood orange, tearing the dark red flesh from the pith with my teeth. Outside, the wind stings my eyes. The first magnolia petals are starting to fly off the trees.

On my way home from work, I buy a houseplant that opens its pink-veined leaves during the day and closes them at night, furling in on itself, making its limbs smaller in the dark. I learn that when plants do this it is called *nyctinasty*. It's a circadian rhythmic movement in response to the onset of darkness. The plant's light receptors in its skin, called phytochromes, cause the petals or foliage to curl inwards, as if asleep. Crocuses do this; as do lotuses, hibiscus, tulips and poppies. The exact reason for nyctinastic movement hasn't yet been determined, but it could be the plant's way of protecting itself from night-time predators, or conserving energy, or both. I watch my plant closely. It is a *Calathea ornata*, native to Colombia and Venezuela, part of a family of plants called *prayer plants* because of the way their leaves and leaflets rise up at dusk as if in prayer.

My anger has nowhere to go. It silently opens and closes inside me.

Second Lunar Month

春分 *spring equinox ~ season of white lilies*

On the day of the Christchurch terrorist attack, because I'm so far away and don't know what else to do, I cut the last two daffodils still alive and bring them with me to place in front of New Zealand House in the middle of London, where piles of flowers and cards and little flags have accumulated on either side of the glass doors: small mountains of grief.

On my way to the vigil at the New Zealand War Memorial that evening, I see flowers everywhere. A man on the train has a single white iris poking out of the pocket of his jeans. I'm holding a bunch of violet-coloured sweet peas that I bought at the flower stall near Embankment right after work. As I often do when I'm on the train at rush hour, I think about what it would be like if something catastrophic happened just then. All the petals would fly up into the air and stay there, suspended, like in a movie. I step off the train at Hyde Park station and almost collide with a girl on the platform cradling a giant bouquet of white lilies in her arms. They dwarf her, giving the impression that she is wearing a cloud of lilies. In that moment, I understand that if I follow her she'll take me exactly where I need to be.

London commuters stare at us and our armfuls of flowers as we carve a sweet-scented path through the crowded station entrance, walking against the current of the city to join the others. We find them standing huddled on the grass around more valleys of flowers, arms around each other, singing quietly, cheeks lit by electric candles flickering in the loud night.

Fourth Lunar Month

清明 *pure brightness ~ season of koru ferns*

Mum and Dad's seaside garden in Wellington is made up of plants inherited from the house's previous owners and ones added by Mum over the years. It's beautiful in a patchwork sort of way, the product of several families' hopes and dreams layered on top of each other. We had been left a giant aloe facing the sea, its red tentacles rising towards the sun; an old pōhutukawa that'd been chopped back too far; dark purple hydrangeas; a slender apple tree; an unruly and abundant feijoa, and a golden kōwhai. By the gate, one or two spring onions burst forth from the earth every spring – we don't know how long ago they were planted there, but we always snip them with scissors to put in our soup noodles. There was a withering wisteria above the deck that couldn't withstand the gale, which Dad replaced with a bougainvillea that occasionally spits mouthfuls of magenta blooms. On week-ends Mum is on her knees in the wet grass, composting and potting up new succulents, collecting fallen feijoas and lemons. While Dad is out walking the dog, Mum follows him on to the beach to collect shell fragments from the shore, spreading them between the plants to create a bed of seashells.

I begin to have recurring dreams of a garden that partly resembles this one, but contains plants from various other landscapes I've known before: a giant yùlán magnolia with creamy basketball-sized flowers, a fig tree, pink peonies. In the dream I'm standing in the doorway of a high-ceilinged house looking up at the terraced garden, where a tall rosemary bush with bright purple flowers grows in the middle. There are furred peaches hanging from low trees, giant orange-and-black butterflies hovering above hydrangeas, some with parts of their wings missing. There is a kōwhai, a lemon tree and a red aloe.

Kiri Piahana-Wong is a poet of Ngāti Ranginui, Chinese and Pākehā ancestry. Her poem 'Day by Day' tracks a series of solitary moments spent in the kitchen and in the garden:

    (iii)
    At home, in the garden.
    My fingers cup the dirt,
    pull up weeds, weigh

and scour. It is mid-
afternoon.

Early evening reading
manuscripts. I reach
through the pages,
pluck out a koru fern.
It needs water, it needs
nurturing. That's why
I am here.

To garden is to care for, to feed, to *tend*: to offer up your
own tenderness to the earth. Some days, in this other
island country, which is the furthest point from the island
where I was born, I think this is why I am here.

20/5/18
In my head I'm planning and planting an
imaginary garden, one made up of all the
gardens I've ever known.

Fifth Lunar Month

小满 *a small fullness ~ season of birds flying homewards*

To find a new poetic lineage I must draw a line diagonally across the Pacific Ocean. I begin with a slim book I checked out from the library, *Women of the Red Plain: An Anthology of Contemporary Chinese Women Poets* translated by Julia C. Lin. I flick through the poems, searching for traces of the familiar. Mei Shaojiang, a poet of Shaanxi Province, measures time in things cultivated from the earth:

> Days are garlic and wild scallions, still
>   sprinkling loose dirt,
> Days are newly rolled up hemp ropes, still
>   damp with water.

In the days after the incident in the lamplit living room, I became increasingly attentive to the needs and rhythms of my balcony garden. I set seedlings on one of Po Po's floral-patterned plastic trays on the windowsill and watched

them obsessively. I measured time according to each centi-
metre of growth. I watched the petals of daffodils turn to
papery husks. I let them wilt and soften in their damp beds.

I decided to attempt my own translation of part of a
poem in the book, one by Bing Xin 冰心, titled 'Paper
Boats' ('纸船'). Bing Xin was born in 1900 in Fujian
Province, one of several regions from which Hakka people
originally come. I created this translation in order to
bring myself closer to Bing Xin and her distant dream-
scape of mountains and sea. I longed to get closer to the
language, one I've always carried with me but lost pieces
of over the years.

母亲，倘若你梦中看见一只很小的白船儿，
不要惊讶它无端入梦。
这是你至爱的女儿含着泪叠的，
万水千山
求它载着她的爱和悲哀归去。

mother, if you see a little white boat
in your dream
don't be startled
it is full of your daughter's tears
it travels across ten thousand waves
to carry her heart
home to you

I slowly, carefully unfold Bing Xin's paper boat, add my own translation to the many already in existence, then refold it and release it into the body of water that is closest to me now.

Ache

A Swimming Diary

Hampstead Heath

1 October
Water temperature: sixteen degrees, according to the
chalkboard. A lifeguard watches from one end; a blue
heron watches from the other. The heron presides over
the pond from her perch just beyond the boundary line
at the far end. All the women climbing into the water
look as if they are swimming towards her, and in a way
we are.

Without realising it, I've become stronger. After a
summer's worth of swimming I can swim the pond's full
length now without pausing to catch my breath. A woman
with a long-legged bird (a heron?) tattooed on her left
ankle rises from the ladder after me and smiles, shivering.

She knows what I know: that the cold pond gives us an invisible superpower that we carry inside us for the rest of the day. Clouds pass across the sun; the wind picks up.

4 October
I undress fast enough so that I can still feel damp sweat on my back from the walk uphill. I lower my body into the water quickly, not thinking too much. I have recently discovered that I'm often capable of doing things that scare me if I don't think too much. As my feet touch the pond I feel the sharp pain of the two-degree drop since my last swim. Pushing out, the ache in my fingers and toes is almost unbearable – and then suddenly it isn't anymore. I have broken through it, out the other side, where there's no more pain.

Afterwards, a woman sits on the bench opposite me eating a pear and wearing only her bra, knickers, socks and a woolly hat. I sit eating my apple and sipping hot water from my yellow thermos, having just pulled on my comfiest jeans, boots, two Uniqlo Heat-Tech thermal tops and my quilted cotton jacket.

7 October
Thirteen degrees means numbness at first. The pain takes a little while to take hold. I'm ten strokes out before I

feel it in my fingers, mostly between the first and second knuckle. If the pain had a colour it would be a hot violet ache, purple with hard edges. On her break, one of the lifeguards cuts a gliding backstroke down the centre of the pond and for a moment we're the only human creatures in the water. It begins to rain soft droplets on my neck and shoulders. I wonder what the difference is between the temperature of pond water and the temperature of a raindrop. I wonder how long it takes for a raindrop to warm up once it hits my skin.

Walking home in the wet floating mist, I hear the sound of a clarinet coming from inside the church on my street. The clarinet player is practising their scales; the bright notes chime through the rain like bells. A small girl and her mum take cover under the eaves. 'Rain, rain, go away,' she sings.

8 October
My fingers sift through red and gold leaves under the surface. A leaf brushes my foot as I kick out and, as usual, I push away the thought that it might be something other than a sturdy leaf. There are ducks and moorhens and two women swimming in their woolly hats. I swim my usual small star-shaped lap around half of the pond, my boundaries marked by the life rings. I remember the first time I saw a moorhen here, and how I stopped in

my tracks; how they look so like the pūkeko of Aotearoa, with their royal blue breast feathers and red beaks.

Over my post-swim cup of ginger tea, I scroll through the news on my phone and read a headline: 'Humpback whale spotted swimming in River Thames'. Flashes of my dream last night suddenly come back to me. An enclosed body of water, a storm, a wooden boat, a grey whale breaching between slow waves.

10 October
The blue heron and black cormorant stand opposite each other on the life rings. I swim out between them and we all make eye contact, then look away. The cormorant shakes its leathery wings and holds them outstretched, facing me. Just like the shags perched along Wellington's south coast, with their wings held up to the wind as if they were imagining how to fly.

A heron in flight is a small winged dinosaur, all elbows and spiked wings. It unfolds its body and swings up and out of the reeds, unbalanced like a marionette.

Someone said that the whale in the river was a wondrous thing, a sign we hadn't ruined everything yet. I knew that wasn't true. By the afternoon it had died. At first I couldn't look at the photograph above the article headlined 'Humpback whale found dead in Thames hit by ship'. Later, I couldn't stop looking at it: a body the size of a truck, bent backwards, being lifted out of the river and into the sky. The air where it should not be. All its dark blueness exposed, still wet.

15 October
My first sunlit swim since September. The water is the clearest I've ever seen. My arms and hands stretch out in front of me, pale gold, inked with the shadows of leaves.

Occasionally, I'm not the only Asian woman at the pond. And I'm not the first Asian woman to write about this place; Ava Wong Davies and Jessica J. Lee are two writers whose descriptions of the Ladies' Pond I read long before I first swam here. In *Turning*, Lee writes: 'I began to swim there alone, surrounded by women who seemed stronger than me. I wanted to be like them: sturdy, no-nonsense, unsentimental.'

In the shower, leaves and silt slide off my skin onto the blue tiled floor.

17 October
Today, a whale fall was discovered more than 10,000 feet deep off the coast of California. The whale fall's discovery

was live-streamed by the Deep Sea Cam on board the *Nautilus*, a boat operated by the Ocean Exploration Trust. A whale fall is created when a whale's carcass floats down to the abyssal zone and lays to rest on the seafloor. As the whale decomposes it transforms into a feeding ground for an ecosystem of deepwater organisms, some of which are bioluminescent.

What does the bottom of the pond look like? The cormorants know. They slip under and leave circles of stillness on the surface that slowly disappear, erasing any trace of the point where their bodies entered the water. As I swim, my eyes are level with diving cormorants and with raindrops hitting the surface, exploding like stars.

21 October

It's the first day of my period and the first day the water temperature dips below twelve. The boundary line has been pulled in, making the swimming area half its usual length. Now there are few who linger after their swim, setting off instead down the wooded track wrapped in scarves and beanies.

Cyclamens are popping up in the undergrowth, though it feels far too early for them. Cyclamens range from frost-tender to frost-hardy; from cream to dark pink. They were the first flower I saw in London after a winter of hardly any colour at all. They spring up from their nests of leaves and unfold their petals from a tight chrysalis, like pink moths. Raindrops cling to the undersides of their wings.

I think of this time of year as *deep autumn* – shēnqiū 深秋 – and I'm now beginning to think of myself as an autumn swimmer. *Cyclamen hederifolium* are autumn-blooming. I was born during the southern hemisphere autumn. But these days, where does autumn begin and end? I catch myself clinging to these old markers of seasonal change while trying to track the shifting pattern of new extremes. April heatwaves, October frosts. I submerge myself in cold water and my body comes up burning.

22 October

A temperature of ten degrees in the water means the lifeguards stand on the deck asking swimmers whether they've swum recently, encouraging them to go slow. The surface glistens. The water is dark and silken, yet somehow also made of a thousand tiny shards of glass that squeeze and cut against my arms and hands. I measure my breathing. The pain gives way faster than expected, transforming into something smooth, shining, weightless. I almost turn back but swim out for one more length instead, just to stay in this velvety in-between state a moment longer, before the cold starts to bite into the centre of my chest, which is when I'll start shaking from the inside out.

Chatting to the lifeguard, I tell her I'm not sure I'm tough enough to keep going into winter. She rolls her eyes at me. 'Look, if you can do twenty degrees, you can do one degree. Just come. Just keep coming,' she says. I want to have as much faith in my body as she does.

She pauses. 'Listen. The kingfisher.' I listen. I've never seen a kingfisher before, but I can hear it: a single high-pitched note, like a bell. She points to a gap between two silver birches where the kingfishers nest. I stare into the trees, hoping to see a flash of turquoise, but between the leaves everything is still.

Another woman, half undressed, listens in. 'How do you know when to get out?'

She sighs. 'When you start to feel wonderful, get out. Everyone's body is different. Here, you'll learn the limits of your own body. But *euphoria is hypothermia.*'

At her words, I realise I've come to know my limits. I know the amount of time it will take for pain to bloom into pleasure. I've come to expect the voice that says:

just a little longer. But *a little longer* is what it could take for shock to kick in. Once a swimmer's misjudged their limit and stayed in too long, they can't lift themselves up the ladder. 'We try not to let you reach that point. Once you do, we just shout at you until you get yourself up and out.'

Wellington Harbour

31 October
Getting off the plane at Wellington Airport, everything is too bright. Hot blue sky, platinum sun, glowing hills covered in tree ferns. My eyes aren't used to this pure, undiluted sunlight. The surface of the sea gleams and I can't look directly at it.

My current visa's expiry date looms. In order to live any longer in England, the only option for me was to fly home and apply from here. While I wait for the outcome, each morning I visit Toby, who's been living with another family in our old house since my parents moved overseas. We go down to the beach and he happily trots into the sea, dunking his nose in the waves. When he's looking tired, we wander back and sunbathe on the grass. I pick lemons off the tree while tūī swoop noisily overhead.

Before leaving London it helped me to think of this trip as a brief in-between period of my life. As if by naming my reality I might feel less adrift. Once the visa appointment was over, all I had to do was wait – it could take anywhere from two weeks to three months, they said. But now that my parents have left, without a physical home to return to, I feel like I'm floating and empty. I fight to keep my anxiety from bubbling over into raw panic. I try to focus on the things I know are real: the garden, a little wild now, is still a place I know by heart. The beach across the walkway is just the same, and so is Toby, apart from speckles of grey fur around his brown eyes.

Two twelve-hour flights mark the shift from the deepening cold of autumn to the slow warmth of spring. My body quickly adjusts, leaning into the hard northerly wind as soon as I get to the coast. I focus on swimming: I replace my routine of swimming in the pond with swimming in the harbour, which feels much more natural to me, to be in constant motion in the tide's swells. I tell myself I'll keep moving. I'll keep swimming, I'll keep writing.

There are two things that make up a Wellington spring: cold wind and hard sun. I feel them both as I undress behind the bus shelter at Lowry Bay. A man walking a cocker spaniel stares at me like I'm insane. The tide is so low I have to wade far out, my body exposed to the wind, waves sucking at my ankles. When I'm waist-deep I dive under. It's cold but an unexpectedly soft kind of cold, gently prickling my skin. I swim parallel to the shore's perfect curve. I am the only creature in the bay.

3 November

When picking Tip Top ice cream flavours, I alternate between three: cookies and cream, chocolate, and boysenberry ripple. Today is a boysenberry ripple kind of day, sharp on the tongue. My cheeks are sore from walking into the wind. Oriental Bay is packed with sunbathers, though only a handful brave the rough water. The sand, imported from Golden Bay, is grainy between my toes. My friend Ella and I smear sunscreen on our shoulders and then she runs ahead of me towards the jade-coloured sea. I skip towards her and we dive into green waves, three to four feet high above our heads, rocking our bodies. London and Wellington are in opposite seasons but somehow the temperatures of the pond and the sea feel almost the same. There's no need to swim; the waves pull me up and down between their crests, flying and falling. 'This is one of the best things about being alive,' Ella yells above the noise.

深 means *deep*, as in the depth of a colour or the depth of the sea. The water is indigo in parts, pea green in others. Ella tells me to look down: layers of sand are rippling and shimmering beneath the surface, moving with the waves and the light. 深秋 *deep autumn*; 深春 *deep spring*.

5 *November*

This beach, where Toby and I have been swimming since we were both small, has always felt like its own ecosystem. It's different from the rest of the coastline, the quiet bays sloping away from the wind. The stretch of shingle between the sea wall and the tide is vast, at least two hundred metres wide. The beach drops down a few steps from the water, a bank of driftwood and rocks to be clambered over.

After rain, when the stormwater ponds fill up, ducks take up residency here, joining the oystercatchers, gulls, shags, sparrows and banded dotterels. There are signs warning dog walkers that this is a nesting ground for kororā, little blue penguins, the smallest penguin in the world. This beach is full of life: native flax, purple daisies, hardy succulents, spiky shrubs with yellow flowers, bees, cabbage butterflies.

It's blowing a northerly gale and Toby insists on taking me to the beach. I throw driftwood for him as we tumble across the rocks, mussel and pāua shells crackling underfoot. Toby runs head first into the waves, ears flapping.

I strip down to my togs and follow him in. An adolescent gull with grey spotted cheeks hovers nearby, eyeing us from up high. I call out to Toby, who's snuffling a clump of kelp, and we make our way back up the beach, stumbling in the pebble drifts as if wading through snow.

6 *November*

In the bay at high tide, I can hop down straight into the water from the bench behind the bus stop. I didn't think I was brave enough to swim today, but then the sun slipped out from behind a green ridge. Efforts to keep my belongings dry are useless; waves wash over my tattered canvas sneakers. Next to the bench, someone has left a large crumbling rock with semi-calcified mussel shells dangling from it.

I need to get under as fast as I can. If I go slow, I'll think too much about the slippery uneven rocks and the rows of cars passing by the beach. The cold grips me roughly at first, then lusciously.

8 *November*

I bunch up my socks and tuck them into my boots beneath the driftwood bench. This broad stretch of Eastbourne Beach curves in a concave shape towards the harbour, jutting out into the wind, which blows in cold and fast. This is total exposure. The wind whips my hair around my neck. I know the waves are stronger than they look.

In this weather, I am always looking for orca. Under pearl-grey clouds every shadow and crinkle on the surface looks like the shape of a marine mammal. I follow the dark shapes closely until my eyes hurt from the effort of focusing. The sea lifts me up and tosses me gently back against the shore as if to say hello, goodbye.

In the afternoon, several friends send me messages with links to the same news article:

> Three orca have been spotted around Wellington Harbour. This morning, keen-eyed residents around Eastbourne, on the eastern shore of the harbour, could see the orca in the shallower waters closer to shore.

12 November
I am the only person in Days Bay. The sea is blue and sequinned like a mermaid's tail. Standing in the morning sun in my yellow high-waisted bikini, painted all over with sunscreen, I feel suddenly bold and brash like the character Stanley from 'At the Bay', written by Katherine Mansfield in 1922 about this very spot. At first light Stanley plunges in triumphantly – 'First man in as usual! He'd beaten them

all again.' First woman in, I dive and swoop in the crushed velvet surf. I come up swaying, shining. The sun's tricked me into thinking I can't feel the cold, but I know my limits. From the shore I look back to the waves, trying to regain my breath, shielding my eyes from the light.

Later, in a bookshop, I hunt for a copy of Mansfield's stories to reread 'At the Bay' while leaning against one of the shelves. In the voice of an omniscient narrator, Mansfield surveys the dawn making its way slowly across these misty hills above the bay. Then she turns her gaze to the sea itself: 'Now the leaping, glittering sea was so bright it made one's eyes ache to look at it.'

15 November
'Not knowing how long you'll get to stay in the city you want to live in feels like travelling half blind, like sending a sound wave across a canyon,' writes Sharlene Teo. The unknown looms at all times at the edges of my vision: the fragility of a passport, paperwork, post offices, the absurdity of trying to live somewhere so far from this shoreline. So, in this strange blank in-between moment in my life, I swim. I swim to get as close to this sea and sky as my body will let me.

Lion's Head Rock is surrounded by churning waves the colour of chocolate milk. Toby watches me wearily as I undress in the wind and drape my clothes over the drift-wood. I dip down below the sand shelf and feel the sharp pull of the undertow. I have never been caught in a rip, but I wonder if at first it feels like this: the way the water moves rapidly beneath the surface, pulling my legs in a different direction to my arms, bending my knees backwards. When a wide wave rolls over the top of me I push my body up to meet it, letting it carry me back to the shore. The undercurrent signals to me I shouldn't venture out further, though the cold is shimmering and spiky on my skin.

Later, drying off in the garden, camellias and peach roses sway in the gale. I pick a wind-fallen pink camellia from the gravel path and place it inside the pages of my note-book, making a mental note to show my mum the next time I see her, whenever that may be.

Tofu Heart

'刀子嘴巴'

I wake before dawn and feel around for my phone next to me. Half asleep, I scroll automatically through updates of lockdown life back home, which looks much the same as always: hot pink sunsets, home-baked hot cross buns, bright crescent moons above the sea at dusk. I am longing now more than ever to touch the sea, or even just to be within sight of the sea for a moment: for some small reminder that it's still there, that I am still surrounded by water.

My friend Rose has posted a picture of a bowl of fresh, homemade dòufu huā 豆腐花, with yóutiáo 油条, fried dough sticks. I hold my finger down on the screen to stop the image from disappearing, a pang of hunger in my belly. I can see the tofu's wobbly texture; I can feel the shape of the soft curds in my mouth. I think of that day I spent with Rose many summers ago in Wellington, swimming in the warm harbour, then walking up through town to our favourite noodle shop. We sat by the window sipping soy milk from little cartons.

豆花

If I translate dòufu huā into English, it loses some of its taste and shape. The direct translation is *tofu flower*, and in Beijing they call it dòufunǎo, *tofu brain*. In English you could call it 'soft bean curd' or even 'jellied tofu', as my dictionary app suggests. 'Tofu pudding' is the one translation that makes sense to me, owing to the dish's custard-like texture.

In Shanghai I lived down the road from a small eatery that served breakfast all day: spring onion oil noodles, deep-fried sesame balls, dòufu huā. I went there often on my own. Their chilli oil glowed fluorescent orange, the colour of a Shanghai summer night. Tender layers of tofu floated in the bowl in the shape of a wide open peony. I remember sitting inside by the window, my damp umbrella on the floor under the table, when another downpour came. Within minutes the gutters flooded again. And then it was all over, the street lit up by the reflections of traffic lights in shallow puddles.

豆浆

In March, one of my last meals before London went into lockdown was at Far East on Gerrard Street. I had been trying to get to Chinatown as often as possible; I'd heard from friends that the whole area had gone eerily quiet. Far East is a little cramped, cash only, and the only place I've found that serves hot dòujiang, soy milk and dòuhuā at all hours of the day.

The air outside is sharp but no longer cold enough for my scarf and gloves, which I shove into the pockets of my coat. I'm served the biggest yóutiáo I've ever seen; I have to rip it in half with my hands before lifting the pieces with my chopsticks. I tuck my hair behind my ears before lifting the bowl of dòuhuā to my lips. The ends of my hair are coarse and splitting from the dry winter air. I think of my first winter in London, two years ago, when I ventured out to try and get to know the city, to try and summon the courage to eat out alone.

Last week a white relative posted a racist meme in our family WhatsApp group. I was already exhausted from pandemic-related anxiety; I didn't have the energy to respond. Some other family members scolded him privately, and later that night I typed out a brief reply: 'This is not OK.' There was no response, though the message was seen.

I hadn't written anything in my invisible document since the previous year, and I thought of opening it, but didn't – rather than quickly noting down what happened and pushing it out of my mind, I felt strong enough this time to slowly consider the implications of the casual comment, and the uncomfortable fact that it came from within my own extended family. I still don't know why they decided to take a screenshot from Facebook, save it to their phone, upload it to WhatsApp and hit 'send'. I don't know how a global pandemic seems to have given new confidence to those who privately, or unconsciously, find racism deeply amusing, and have never been forced to confront this fact about themselves. Moments when I stayed quiet, when I was younger and didn't know what to say, still haunt me.

豆腐

The Cambridge dictionary definition of tofu reads: 'a soft, pale food that has very little flavour but is high in protein, made from the seed of the soya plant'. I feel sad for the person who wrote this. Many people wrinkle their noses at the mention of bean curd and I get flustered when this happens. My cheeks grow hot, I wave my arms in lieu of words.

Bean curd is one of my favourite names in English. It's firm on the outside but soft in the middle, where the springy mouthfeel of *bean* blends with the warm liquid *curd*. In Mandarin, too, 'dòufu' is composed of soft sounds. But to say the word requires a gentle bite, the tip of your tongue touching the back of your teeth.

豆腐皮

Today I'm dreaming of a particular dish: jiācháng dòufu, *home-style tofu*, at Red Hill, a Sichuan restaurant on Manners Mall in Wellington. When I was at university we'd go there for the dumplings and the karaoke: Christina Aguilera's first two albums interspersed with Mandarin pop. The deep-fried tofu cubes have a chewy skin that absorbs the black bean sauce.

There's a famous Hakka dish of braised tofu cubes stuffed with pork: niàng dòufu. Mum says Po Po used to make it a lot. I remember Po Po placing it in the centre of the table in one of her blue-rimmed serving dishes with slender fish painted on the sides. The tofu wobbled strangely under the warm lamp.

豆腐饭

In Mandarin class we studied Chinese funeral practices, which are numerous and still unfamiliar to me, since I've never attended a funeral of a Chinese family member of mine. The traditional vegetarian funeral banquet is some-times called the dòufufàn, the *tofu meal*. We learned that tofu is often given as an offering because it's soft enough to be swallowed by a ghost.

It's Qīng Míng today, Tomb-Sweeping Festival, but many families all over the world cannot gather to mourn their dead.

豆泡

To make dòuhuā at home you need just three ingredients: water, soybeans and a coagulant, most commonly gypsum powder, which sets the soy milk into tofu. According to Andrea Nguyen, the author of *Asian Tofu*, gypsum produces 'loftier curds'. Normally I'd look on eBay, but I feel guilty buying non-essential things online during lockdown, so I opt for one of Nguyen's suggested alter-natives: lemon juice.

In the back of my mind I feel a grinding pressure to write, to create, to make good use of this time. But my body feels worn down, my nerves softened and tenderised.

I have never held a soybean in my palm until today. It is round, smooth and a creamy pale gold in colour. Huáng dòu 黄豆 – *yellow bean*.

黄豆

On the eighteenth day of lockdown, I put one cup of soybeans in a bowl to soak overnight. Soaking is one of the most magical and satisfying processes in cooking, and one I've rarely had the time and patience for until now. In the morning the yellow beans were swollen, splitting cleanly in half when I squeezed them between my fingers. While they simmered gently for forty minutes, the kitchen filling up with steam, I rolled out the dough for spring onion pancakes – something crisp to dip into my dòuhuā.

To transform dòujiang into dòuhuā (from *milk* into *flower*), a few teaspoons of lemon juice is all it takes. The recipe instructs me to cover the pot and wait one hour for the dòuhuā to set, but I can't stop myself from peeking. Eventually the skimmed surface of the milk begins to change: shimmering, wobbling. Sitting on the kitchen floor waiting for my phone timer to buzz, I scroll through Twitter, where I see images of people in Beijing standing metres apart holding yellow chrysanthemums in their hands, their heads bowed.

'豆腐心'

There's a Chinese proverb: '刀子嘴, 豆腐心.' It means, literally, *knife mouth, tofu heart*. In other words, *sharp-tongued but soft-hearted*.

My dòuhuā's curds are not lofty, nor do they float in perfect petalled layers. But they have set a little, which is something. The taste is more sour than regular tofu. There's still that beany richness on my tongue.

I ladle the soupy pudding into a rice bowl and sprinkle it with dark brown sugar and a little fresh ginger – my lazy version of 'ginger-infused sugar syrup', which I've run out of energy to make. Today, I need something sweet and soft. I take a picture and post it in the family chat.

豆腐衣

Against a backdrop of misty mountains and pomelo trees, a young woman with braided hair uses a scythe to harvest soybeans from the fields near her home. This is Li Ziqi, the Chinese YouTube celebrity whose soothing, ethereally beautiful videos of cooking meals with fresh ingredients from her garden have garnered her many millions of followers. Her on-screen garden, located in the mountains of rural Sichuan Province, is like a dreamworld. Impossibly lush, it sparkles and pulses with life like a scene from a Ghibli movie, in high-definition. Magnolia trees with pink blooms, red chillies, crimson climbing roses, glistening lime and lemon trees. The changing colours of her garden show the altered passage of time: her soybeans are sown on

Qīng Míng, in the middle of spring, and harvested at the autumn equinox.

In lockdown, the patterns of each day blur into the next. I watch these videos obsessively in between hours of writing and working from home. Outside, it rains like I've never known it to rain in London before: violent downpours that last only minutes, followed by warm, drizzling rain. The soft sounds of Li Ziqi's garden begin to blend with the sounds of my blue kitchen, which is the place where I've managed to hold on to some sense of normalcy: raindrops on the windows, soy milk simmering on the stove, the kettle boiling on the counter. All the blossoms have fallen, and the plums and apricots in the allotments by the park are beginning to soften.

三点水

Wellington, 1996

Begin in a small room with banana-coloured walls. Begin by drawing hearts and stars on a sheet of paper, not listening to the teacher's sing-song voice. All around you on the walls are bright posters with pictures of animals, colours, fruits.

Begin with the soothing language of apple juice, rice cakes and steamed dim sum. Begin with a handful of words in dialect – Hakka and Cantonese sprinkled with English.

You try to keep up with everyone else. You can never remember the hand signs quickly enough. Seven 七: press your thumb and two fingers together in the shape of a bird! Eight 八: hold your thumb to the sky, point out your finger! Nine 九: curve your finger in the shape of a worm!

Begin with six basic radicals which are the foundations of many Chinese characters: person, knife, mouth, roof, heart, water. The last one, water, is written as 氵. It's known as 三点水, or *three drops of water*.

水		shuǐ		water; a body of water			
水果		shuǐ	guǒ	fruit			
水饺		shuǐ	jiǎo	boiled dumplings			

~

The first words were carved in shell and bone. Oracle bone script (甲骨文, literally *shell-bone script*) was the language of pyromancy – divination by fire. Fortune tellers inscribed questions for the gods on pieces of ox bone and turtle shell. They heated the fragments over a flame until the fragments cracked from the heat. Their answers lay in the pattern of splits and fissures in burnt bone.

In these earliest confirmed examples of Chinese script, which date back three thousand years to the late Shang dynasty, there are two forms of language at play: one in the familiar pictographic symbols that resemble the hànzi we know today, and one in the cracks between the lines of text.

The oracle bone ideograms are very early versions of today's Chinese characters, but many have still not yet been deciphered. The shapes look ancient but familiar, a little crooked and spindly like my own handwriting as a child. One closely resembles its modern counterpart: a circle with a dot in the centre, a sun 日.

Shanghai, 2006

Every weekend during the long hot summer, you walk fifteen minutes down the road to the language school housed in an apartment complex on the corner of Anfu Lu and Wulumuqi Lu. The plane trees' wide leaves tremble above the footpath.

The July heat makes the air feel pressurised, combustible. It presses against your skin until you get to the windowless room, where icy air-conditioned wind blows down your neck. Today, for your second lesson, your Mandarin tutor is teaching you how to write your name for the first time. She helps you break each character down into four separate parts. Sun, moon. Tooth, bird. You connect each shape together awkwardly. Your fingers feel clumsy, pressing down too hard on the thin gridded paper.

You can never remember the correct stroke order, and drawing them doesn't come naturally to you. Your characters are childlike, ungraceful. They slant too far to the right just like your English handwriting does. There's something your body still needs to learn, or unlearn.

You write them over and over again until all the curves and lines begin to blur together. *Bird, sun, tooth, moon.*

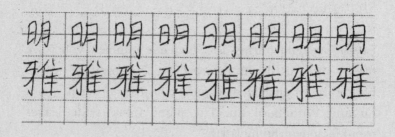

~

Nǔshū 女书 – *women's script* – is a writing system that was used by women in rural Hunan Province up until the early 1900s. I first stumbled across a mention of Nǔshū online in 2017, when I was studying in Shanghai. The symbols partly resembled characters I knew, but tilted and stretched into strange, slender shapes. Their curved strokes made them look like long-legged pond-skimming insects, as if alive, about to lift up off the page in flight.

Unlike Chinese, a logographic script where each character represents a word or part of a word, Nǔshū is a syllabic script – each character is a single syllable spoken aloud.

Women and girls wrote to each other in Nǚshū, often embroidering the words onto blankets, clothing and little clothbound booklets. The last person known to be fully proficient in Nǚshū, a woman named Yang Huanyi, passed away in 2004.

Writers and scholars have been fascinated by Nǚshū ever since it came to light. I became obsessed. The idea of a script devised by women exclusively for other women felt mythical, mystical. When they came of age, girls would be taught Nǚshū by their aunts, and they would be assigned a lǎotóng 老同, a *sworn sister* of the same age, with whom they'd sign a pact of sisterhood. I pictured girls and women writing notes to each other by firelight, or threading songs and stories from their lives onto hand-woven cloth.

In Lisa See's historical novel *Snow Flower and the Secret Fan*, the two main characters, named Lily and Snow Flower, are sworn sisters who write letters to each other in Nǚshū on paper fans. The 2011 film adaptation directed by Wayne Wang (who also directed *The Joy Luck Club*) inserted a parallel narrative of two women living in contemporary Shanghai, one of whom is Snow Flower's great-great-granddaughter. Inspired by the story of their ancestors' friendship, one night they sign a pact on the cover of their favourite Faye Wong album.

Journalist and academic Ilaria Maria Sala, who has studied
Nǔshū for many decades, has spoken out against the way
Nǔshū has been sensationalised in popular culture as a
secret language of women's suffering and pain. Sala's
fieldwork in Hunan revealed to her that Nǔshū was much
more complex; it was both the language of rituals and
the language of everyday life. Rather than a secret spoken
language between women, it merely transcribed the local
Jiangyong dialect, and it wasn't kept secret from men.

Nǔshū script is becoming more widely accessible online.
There's now a free online dictionary based on the original
Dictionary of Nǔshū Standard Characters compiled by
Gong Zhebing and Tang Gongwei. On the screen, I input
the two characters of my name.

明　雅

Wellington, 2011

'Nǐ wèishéme xuéxi zhōngwén?' 'Why are you studying
Mandarin?' The question comes up at the beginning of

each new semester. Your mostly male classmates all have very practical, career-driven motives for picking the subject: 'To do business in China.' 'To become a Chinese translator.' 'To study international relations.' When a mature student makes a crass joke about wanting a Chinese girlfriend, the teacher laughs it off. When it's your turn, you mumble something about wanting to learn more about Chinese culture, as if that culture wasn't also your own.

The university buildings are perched on a steep hill above the city. From the fifth floor of the library, you can see out over the whole blue harbour. Ferries passing each other on their way in and out, planes coming in unsteadily to land in the wind, small white lighthouses on the edge of the south coast. On a clear day, you can see white-capped mountains watching over the city from a distance.

In August it snowed at sea level. It was the first time you or anyone you know had ever seen snow in Wellington, where winters bring freezing rain and wind, but never snow. It started during an art history lecture on the Pre-Raphaelites – Ophelia's drenched hair floating on a PowerPoint slide in the lecture hall – when someone glimpsed what looked like snow out of the upper windows and whispers went round the rows. There were at least two hundred students enrolled in first-year art history, so you often used the time to practise Chinese characters in the back row, unseen. As soon as class ended you rushed out to the quad, where everyone was standing around laughing and looking up at the sky, holding out their tongues.

Fat flakes fell on the beaches, melting instantly as soon as they touched the waves. In the morning, the hills emerged out of the mist still dusted in sugar. By the afternoon it was gone.

		雨		yǔ				rain				
		雪		xuě				snow				
		港		gǎng				harbour				

~

I met the poet and artist Jen Bervin in Shanghai in 2016. She was in the city for the Shanghai International Literary Festival, where she presented her ongoing collaborative project on the fourth-century poet Su Hui, one of the earliest known Chinese women poets, who is said to have invented the 'multidirectional poem' form. Su composed and embroidered in silk a square poem consisting of 841 characters in a 29 x 29 character grid that can be read in any direction: horizontally, vertically, diagonally. The title of her poem, 'Xuanji Tu'

'璇玑图', refers to an ancient Chinese astronomical instrument, and is variously translated as 'The Star-Gauge Poem' or 'The Map of the Armillary Sphere'. According to legend, Su addressed the poem to her husband, who had left her for a concubine. She sent it to him and he came back to her.

At the poetry reading in a bar overlooking the Huangpu River, the screen behind Bervin showed a digitised version of Su Hui's poem. I could briefly make out a handful of words scattered across the grid: 土 *earth*, 飞 *fly*, 长 *long*, 路 *road*, and in the very centre of the square, a *heart* 心.

Bervin's art often engages with poetry and textiles. In *The Dickinson Composite Series*, the artist embroidered Emily Dickinson's handwritten punctuation marks (as they appear in her original manuscripts, letters and notes) in red thread onto large-scale quilts. For her Su Hui project, Bervin asked three embroiderers from the Suzhou Museum of Embroidery – three women – to embroider Su Hui's poem over the course of a year, using the complex Chinese technique of double-faced stitching on fine silk. A six-minute video shows embroiderer Yu Juan slowly pulling purple thread back and forth through taut fabric, looping fragments of the ancient poem through her fingers.

Years later I came across images online of a vast scroll suspended from the ceiling of a small gallery. On the scroll were painted repeating characters: 去, 门, 嘴. In the middle of the room stood a worktable, a calligraphy brush, a bottle of black ink. The installation is by Rainbow Chan, an Australian interdisciplinary artist whose work brings together translation, calligraphy, traditional craft and installation. The artwork's title, 回 – *To Enclose One's Mouth*, literally describes the character 回 (huí), meaning *to return*: a mouth enclosed within a larger mouth. Chan wrote a poem in English, then used Google Translate to translate the poem into Chinese. She then painted each character of the transcribed poem ten times on a wide silk scroll, re-enacting her childhood memory of writing and rewriting characters ten times over. The poem reads:

> I try to speak
> but my tongue refuses.
> My mouth is a perfect logogram,
> a frame with no content.

Beijing, 2013

A catalogue of firsts. First time travelling alone, first time walking on a frozen lake, first time ordering food in

Mandarin every day and not having to translate from English first inside your head. You begin to sense a brand-new intimacy with this language you've been trying to get closer to for so long. Words and sentence structures are now closer to where you need them, just under the surface of your skin; you reach for them with little effort, without having to pull them up from the depths.

The city is new to you but feels oddly familiar, like those places that appear and reappear in dreams. This is where your parents first met – there are pictures of this dusty skyline dotted around the house. It's strange piecing together the backdrops of old photos with the real thing: blazing red flags by the gates of the Forbidden City, parched hills unravelling in the distance behind the Great Wall.

Beijing snow feels dry and soft on your cheeks. It gets swept off the road by street cleaners before it has a chance to freeze into black ice. It glows in white drifts beside the footpaths. The air is so dry that the skin around your nails cracks, begins to bleed. When you come in from the cold, everything you touch sparks with static. You have never experienced cold like this before: two thermal layers, two jumpers, two pairs of wool socks, leather gloves borrowed from your mother, a knitted bobble hat, a padded shearling coat.

You go out exploring alone, warding off homesickness by trying lots of local Beijing snacks. You stand in the doorway of Family Mart licking a hard-frozen vanilla ice cream speckled with milk chocolate flakes. You take the subway three stops away to a mall where, according to the guide-book, there's a noodle place known for its roast duck ramen. You sit in a booth sipping the rich broth, balancing half a soy-marinated egg on your spoon. The steam thaws your fingers and cheeks, still red from the cold.

冰			bīng			ice	
冰	淇	淋	bīng	qí	lín	ice	cream
汤			tāng			soup	

~

When I was a teenager my mum took me to the Dowse Art Gallery in Wellington. I was bored, wandering aimlessly around the dark galleries. I found myself in a room surrounded by blue shimmering objects dangling from the ceiling. The shapes shook slightly as I moved closer to them. They were traditional Chinese-style paper-cuts made out of squares of blue translucent plastic: zodiac animals, stars, flowers, familiar Chinese characters.

This was *The Unavailable Memory of Gold Coin Café*, an installation by the artist Kerry Ann Lee, whose parents owned the Gold Coin Café takeaway shop at the top of Willis Street in Wellington when Lee was growing up. The building was deemed an earthquake risk and demolished in 2013. Lee revisited the abandoned site for her research, rediscovering it as a place of distant but living memory. In the accompanying exhibition catalogue created by the artist, various paper ephemera are presented like precious excavated materials: a takeaway menu with prices crossed out in pen, bright red and yellow joss paper, a blurry family photograph.

But these details about Lee's life were unknown to me that day in the gallery. I remember wanting to touch the glittering objects hovering like apparitions. Mum came to find me to tell me we were leaving. For a moment we stood mesmerised by the paper-cuts, the way light shone through them, casting blue shadows onto the floor, the walls, our arms.

Shanghai, 2016

You spend humid afternoons in your dorm room copying words onto flash cards. Twice a week the teacher sets dictation tests and the only way to learn is to write each character at least twenty times until your wrist is sore, until each stroke becomes embedded in muscle memory.

You stick the cards all over the walls above your bed. At night you can see them, illuminated by the soft glow of lights in the windows of dorm buildings opposite.

You duck out between downpours to bike to your closest dumpling restaurant, exercise books stuffed in your backpack. Wonton soup, iced green tea, choi sum leaves steamed with ginger. Pages of gridded paper are spread out on the café table. The heel of your palm is rubbed silver with pencil graphite.

The path to fluency is slippery, unstable. Some words never stick. Every week, hundreds of hànzi float in and out of your memory, leaving parts of themselves behind while others slip into the current.

One afternoon, you're studying in the library along with a hundred others sitting silently at long tables, heads bowed over textbooks, when symphonic music begins to play over the library's speaker system. It starts softly, then swells in volume. You look up, bewildered, and it stops. So brief that some students wearing headphones haven't noticed. Others seem to be pretending nothing happened. A couple of people are giggling, muffling their voices in the folds of their books – the only confirmation you didn't imagine it. You've never heard announcements in the library before, but maybe it was meant to be a campus-wide notice, a technical test, or a failed prank? You didn't recognise the music but maybe it was a well-known piece – someone's favourite song? Out of the tall open windows you notice it's started raining, lightly at first, then building to a downpour. The downpour soon drowns out all other noise.

					a current or stream of water
流		liú			
流利		liú	lì		fluent, smooth
流泪		liú	lèi		to shed tears

~

If someone asked me to draw my languages in the shape of a tree, I'd think of Mandarin and English as twin trunks, with Hakka and Cantonese branching off in either direction. I always thought I had to master Mandarin before I could dream of starting on the others, which are less commonly taught as second language subjects, but now I don't know if this is true.

Dialect: 方音, *regional language*. I used to think of dialects as languages without standardised writing systems, rendering them incomplete, less developed. But a dialect is not just a *regional language*. Dialect is family, is blood, is history. In my family we have Hakka, English, Mandarin and Cantonese. English is the common tongue between us, and the edges of the other languages all melt into the edges of our English.

The standardisation and simplification of the Chinese written script is steeped in a history of revolution, violence and colonisation. There are hundreds of regional Chinese languages connected in some way to Mandarin, known as 'Sinitic' languages, and there are thought to be a further three hundred additional languages currently spoken within mainland China – Tibetan, Mongolian, and Uyghur are the most widely spoken non-Sinitic languages in China.

THE SIX TONES OF THE HAKKA DIALECT

Even 平聲	Going 下聲	Departing 去聲	Entering 入聲
1 Upper even 上平 foù 走		4 Upper departing 上去 foù 父	5 Upper entering 上入 foǔc 復
2 Lower even 下平 foù 湖	3 Going down 下聲 foù 虎		6 Lower entering 下入 foǔc 福

What if dialects are not branches, but roots? Hakka, which I can't speak, is the language that gets shouted the loudest down the phone by our elders. The Hakka people are a migratory subgroup of Han Chinese with a distinctive language and culture of their own. Hakka are believed to have come from the area of central China bordering the Yellow River; they then gradually migrated southwards, spreading the Hakka language and its many regional variants all over the world. Yet it's the least well-known of my four connected languages. It has no formal written script of its own, but instead can be transcribed using traditional Chinese characters.

There are very few words I know in Hakka, all from childhood: *milk*, *sleep*, *bread*. It's through old texts written by European missionaries that I begin to find my way in the dark towards a broader Hakka vocabulary. Swiss missionaries compiled the first Hakka lexicon in 1909, and Presbyterian missionary Donald MacIver published the first Hakka–English dictionary in 1926. A later dictionary, from 1959, compiled by the Italian Jesuit priest Guerrino Marsecano, has been digitised by the National Taichung University of Science and Technology. Each definition includes the word written in simplified Chinese characters and the romanised punctuation, with tone marks.

Marsecano's guide to the six tones is useful to me. My foreign throat and lips aren't used to the shapes – but I feel I can come close to wrapping my tongue around them, since I am at home within Mandarin's four tones. At any rate, six tones seem easier than Cantonese's nine. But Marsecano lived in Hsinchu County, Taiwan, and his Hakka dictionary's pronunciations and tones are particular to that region, and may not necessarily apply to the many variants of Hakka spoken by my relatives in Singapore, Malaysia and Canada.

In Mandarin, the word *fluent*, 流利 liúlì, has the word 流 within it: an adjective, *fluid*, and also a verb, *to flow*. Fluency is not stable; it moves. The written character has water running through it: three curved lines flowing outwards.

SEA (n) hòi 海 ; hòi-yòng (ocean) 海洋；hòi-lòng 海浪; pō-lòng (wave) 波浪.AT — , ts'ái hòi hóng 在海上；hòng hòi tchoūng 航海中 ; mô kât-sât 麻呷殺.BOUNDLESS — , voû piēn t'ái hòi 無邊大海.CALM — , tiām-ts'ín kái hòi 恬靜个海. MEDITERRANEAN — , t'í-tchoūng hòi 地中海.OPEN — , koūng hòi 公海. ROUGH — , hì t'ái lóng kái hòi 起大浪个海.— FOOD , hòi sàn voût 海產物.— PORT , hòi kòng 海港.— POWER , hòi-kiōun lìt 海軍力.TO CROSS THE — , p'iāo yòng kó hòi 漂洋過海. TO TRAVEL BY — , hòng hòi 航海。

~

Japanese artist Tomoko Kawao uses a calligraphy brush almost the size of her own body to create canvasses that take up the floor area of entire rooms. Her practice combines traditional calligraphy, known as shodō 書道

in Japanese, with performance art and installation. Watching a video of one of her performances, I can hear the sound of the end of a rainstorm in the slow drip of ink. The only other sounds are her breathing, and the soft sweeping of her body touching the paper. The characters are borne from her body; her body takes on the shape of her script. In an image posted to Kawao's Instagram page on the 5th of April, 2020, the character 家 – *home* – is painted in black ink against a white background, with the artist herself lying on the canvas, curved across the top in the shape of the roof radical, ⼧. She wears a black top and leggings, her arms crossed over her chest, knees bent. Her long hair sweeps downwards like a brushstroke, or a wave.

London, 2019

You recognise the smell of the calligraphy ink from some room of your childhood: oily and plasticky, reminiscent of acrylic paints. From inside the fluorescent-lit room in the Chinese community centre, you can hear the cold spring rain coming down. The room is sparse, apart from a porcelain vase holding a spray of branches with the orange husks of physalis fruits hanging from them like little paper lanterns. Ferns, vines, aloes and monstera have been placed in every room of the centre, with labels stuck to the pots displaying their Chinese names written in black permanent marker. Physalis, *winter cherry*, 酸浆.

It's your first time holding a calligraphy brush. It feels clumsy in your fist. Your wrist is too tight, your fingers too tense. You are the youngest in the class; four older women sit at desks with their brushes, inks, scrolls and thermoses of tea. They smile brightly, pour tea, offer biscuits, but they aren't interested in where you're from or where you got your scraps of Mandarin. They sit down and get to work, copying out their ancient poems in silence.

Hu Laoshi is a patient, soft-spoken man from Beijing. He explains everything in Mandarin, which means most of the details are lost on you, but your body slowly eases back into the sound and feel of this language you haven't spoken in months. When he touches his ink-dipped brush to the paper, his lines are so fluid and light. He curves the tip to make a swoosh at the edge of each stroke in the shape of a magpie's tail feathers.

Begin by dipping your brush in the water dish, then tipping two or three drops of water into the pooling black ink. Begin with the oldest and simplest of the five calligraphy scripts, 篆书 zhuàn shū, known as *seal script*, not too different from the very first symbols that were carved into bone.

'Xiàn shàng, hòu xià,' Hu Laoshi says. First up, then down. You repeat this to yourself as you begin to paint. He asks for your Chinese name, and shows you what the characters look like in ancient seal script. He slowly draws a new set of shapes, ones you've never seen before.

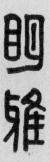

'Fàngsōng fàngsōng bà. Don't rush.' Calligraphy is like doing tai chi, he explains – you need to relax your whole body, from the top of your head to your wrist, down to the tip of your calligraphy brush, which should be an extension of your body.

You try to breathe, letting the brush take you where you need to go. You lean too close over the table, accidentally dipping the ends of your hair in ink, splattering the paper. You hope no one's seen. You quickly tie up your hair, then shake three drops of water into the black ink and begin again.

Museum of White Clouds

One night in a dream, Kerry Ann Lee's father journeyed from Wellington to Xi'an to see the terracotta warriors . . .

Kerry Ann Lee, *Return to Skyland*

IN A DREAM, Po Po takes me to visit the terracotta warriors at Te Papa. They've been flown here from China and put on display in an earthquake-proof case on an earthquake-proof stand, to be gazed at inside an earthquake-proof museum by the sea.

In the dream, I don't just speak her language; I dream in it, too. We both call the same city home. We wait at the bus stop on Kōwhai Street for the number 83 into town. Po Po flashes her Gold Card at the bus driver and her eyes sparkle.

~

We sit by the window and zoom along the Hutt Road looking at the shimmering sea. It's warm for January; Po Po is wearing a cotton T-shirt Mum bought her from Uniqlo in Singapore last Christmas, white with a daisy pattern.

~

We walk to the wharves, bracing ourselves against the wind. Po Po pauses to watch with delight the teenagers cannonballing off the wharf into the harbour. She takes out her phone, which we are still teaching her how to use, and snaps a picture of the splashes.

~

In the dream, we are not the only Chinese people in the queue. We are not even the only half-Chinese-grand-daughter-plus-Chinese-grandma pair in the queue, and we both register this without needing to say anything about it.

~

We walk through dark rooms with gold writing on the walls and stand together in front of the moving picture of Epang Palace with its jade rooftops and white herons and blue clouds drifting across the screen. The clouds and the birds look familiar. 'They look just like the birds that used to visit your garden in K.K.,' I say to her and she nods, 'mmm!' in agreement. 'Are they still there?' I ask. She smiles.

~

I have a real memory of visiting Xi'an with my parents and Po Po and Gong Gong and my cousins and Aunty Bin and Uncle Boon when I was twelve or thirteen, but I don't remember much apart from rows upon rows of empty-eyed heads and horses arranged in formation in a massive pit of dirt. What I remember is the blinding heat – it was mid-July and thirty-nine degrees by mid-morning, which sounded both dramatic and scientific, and which I repeated matter-of-factly to my friends afterwards: 'it was thirty-nine degrees by mid-morning.' Our Converse sneakers kicked up clouds of hot dust that settled on our damp skin. All we wanted was ice cream and air conditioning, and when we finally found it Po Po came and sat with us while the other grown-ups went to explore yet another ancient emperor's ancient tomb.

~

In the dream Po Po leads me into a small room off to one side, filled with a purplish and red light. The walls are covered in a pattern of objects and faces I recognise. I want to reach out and touch them: blue butterflies, a mooncake, a pink peony, a warrior queen, a monkey king, kung fu fighters floating on invisible treetops. I turn to show Po Po this wall covered in what seems to be a repeating pattern of some of my earliest childhood memories, but I find her sitting on a chair, her hands on her knees, her eyes fixed on the screen ahead, where an old-fashioned projector flips images of familiar objects onto the wall. They are objects from another time, things that Po Po might have owned when she was a little girl in China, before she escaped to Malaysia: a faded teacup, a chipped soup spoon, a child's pair of blue silk slippers.

~

I ask her, 'well, what did you think?' over our bowls of roast duck rice noodles at KC Café, where we are sitting at a table by the window. Po Po normally orders off the secret Chinese-only menu but today we want roast duck. A dry, sweeping northerly wind whistles along the thin pane of glass on our left, causing it to vibrate. I understand that this dream is not earthquake-proof. 'Chīfàn ba, chīfàn,' she replies wearily, not quite smiling but her eyes glinting as she holds her chopsticks in one hand

and spoon in the other. She dips her chopsticks into the bowl, swirls, lifts the translucent noodles onto her spoon to form a perfect bite-sized noodle mountain, and begins to eat.

In the Archive of Waterfalls

1. *cloud-forest white*
This is the closest I've been to the summit of the mountain. I'm surrounded by clouds so thick that my parents' outlines grow hazy as they step ahead of me towards the lookout. Beyond them, I can make out the faint edges of a rocky landscape. Tree branches curl out of the whiteness. Here, there's almost no difference between precipitation and cloud, between liquid and air. I walk into the mist and it dampens my skin.

The rainforest looms all around us, vines and pitcher plants spilling over the road. Up here, rain falls persistently all year round. A layer of low cloud touches the treetops, creating a forest canopy heavy with water. Moisture condenses on the leaves and drips down onto everything that lives below, nourishing the wet undergrowth. This type of tropical montane forest is also known as *cloud forest*, *water forest* or *mossy forest*, named for the epiphytes that flourish here: mosses, orchids, algae and ferns, all organisms that feed and grow off the surfaces of other plants.

We are about halfway up Mount Kinabalu, the highest peak in the Malay Archipelago. This is one of the highest points accessible by road, a starting point for climbers to begin their slow ascent to the summit. In the distance, small waterfalls flow from steep heights down into the valleys below like strips of white ribbon stitched onto a dark backdrop. From where I stand, I can see thick clouds of mist at the point where water flows over a rocky cliff edge, altering the speed and shape of the moving body of water, turning a narrow stream into a waterfall. The place where the waterfall begins is somewhere out of sight, high above the cloudline. As the car winds its way up towards the mountain, I trace the thin silvery lines with my eyes until they disappear.

When I was little, I conducted raindrop races from the back seat of the car during long journeys. I'd pick two fat drops falling side by side and trace their progress with my fingertip as they slid down the glass. I stuck my face right up to the window, eagerly awaiting the moment at the end of the race when one raindrop would touch the other and, as if by magic, the two would become one: a tiny waterfall pouring into the crack between the car door and the glass.

We aren't climbers today, only day trippers. We're on a drive organised by Michael, one of Mum's old friends from school. Our itinerary whenever we're in Kota Kinabalu is always dictated by activities planned by my mother's former classmates: an array of chatty aunties and uncles who greet me like we really are family. Michael passes us paper bags of nuts to feed the mountain squirrels. I glance around: no mountain squirrels to be found in the surrounding rocks and trees, which are eerily quiet in the mist. But someone rustles their paper bag and sure enough, small creatures begin to emerge like little long-tailed ghosts. They hop and dangle between the branches of the trees on the other side of the railings as if performing for us tourists.

On the way back home, we take a detour into the mountain foothills to see the *Rafflesia*, the largest flower in the world. *Rafflesia* flowers for only one week of its nine-month life cycle, and only during the rainy season. It begins blooming at night, which also marks the beginning of its death. Almost as soon as it blooms the flower starts to decompose, giving off the rotting scent that earns the plant its other name: corpse flower. The smell attracts the insects that will disperse its pollen.

We traipse single file down a raised walkway beneath the dripping canopy. Dad taps my shoulder and points to a mound on the forest floor beside the walkway. I step closer: what looks like a chunk of darkened flesh is really a giant flower, peach-pink, shiny and unreal like a sci-fi movie prop made of plaster. There's no stench but I detect a sulphurous scent, bittersweet, like liquorice and old cheese. I can just make out the sponge-like skin of its petals, rippling and porous, more reptile than flower.

2. *National Geographic yellow*

We spent so many Christmases at the old house in Kota Kinabalu when we were small. On days when it rained non-stop and we couldn't go to the pool on the hill over-looking the valley, we'd rummage through the boxes and shelves of old books, magazines and photographs that sat untouched in all the upstairs rooms. Mum unearthed an ancient Monopoly set, one she and my aunt remembered playing when they were kids. My cousin Sara brushed the dust off the box and set it on the floor between us. We sat cross-legged in the bedroom that used to belong to my mum, one of two rooms in the old house that has air-conditioning. The humming AC unit blew icy wind down on our necks as we gently opened the cardboard box, which had begun to fall apart at the edges. Inside, though, all the pieces were still there: the little red dice, the pink and yellow slips of paper money which we stacked in neat piles on the floor. We played all afternoon and for hours the next day while the sound of geckoes chirping and dogs barking floated in the air.

When we'd finally had too many days in a row of Monopoly, we lay on the cool varnished floor and flipped through Gong Gong's huge stacks of old *National Geographics*. Gong Gong has a lifelong subscription; every month they keep on coming, fifty years since his first issue. The pages of the oldest copies felt rough and papery, not glossy like those from the last two decades. The signature yellow of their spines had faded to a pale buttery colour. Inside, the pictures were dreamlike and super-saturated: bright blue skies above a sparkling fjord, an erupting volcano covered in fiery lava, a glowing city seen from space.

We turned to the bottom shelf, where Gong Gong kept copies of the books he had published himself. I can see the cover in my mind: a school of colourful fish, gold and silver and mottled red, all swimming towards the book's spine, underneath a title in bold lettering: *The Fresh-Water Fishes of North Borneo* by Robert Inger and Chin Phui Kong. I pulled it from the shelf and held it on my lap, along with a stack of other books with titles like *Marine Invertebrates of Malaysia* and *A Field Guide to Shells and Molluscs of Borneo*. I loved the way these books resembled shopping catalogues, every picture of every species neatly hand-drawn in black-and-white lines, named and labelled underneath. I turned straight to the six or so pages of thick glossy paper in the very middle of the book, where fish with fluorescent yellow spines and blue flowing tails shone in colour photographs.

Chin Phui Kong is Gong Gong, my grandfather, an ichthyologist – a marine biologist who specialises in fish. He was born in Sandakan, Sabah, in 1923. His father and grandfather migrated together to Malaysia from Guangdong in southern China before he was born. He went to secondary school in China, where in 1944 he was recruited to join the army to fight in the resistance movement against the Japanese alongside the British and the Kuomintang as part of Force 136. After the war, he went back to China to study marine biology at Xiamen University, then worked at the Sabah Fisheries Department in Malaysia for the rest of his career.

Gong Gong loves golf, watching the news, Tiger beer, and talking to anyone in great detail about freshwater fishes. He is cheerful and quiet, and can speak Hakka, Mandarin, Cantonese, Malay and English. He's ninety-seven now and I last saw him three years ago. My plans this year to visit him were scuppered, with all borders closed and all flights cancelled, and it's getting harder for him to speak on the phone, especially in English, although Mum explains to him a little about my writing projects. Each week he tells her what he's seen on the news, repeats his astonishment that there are people in America still voting for Trump.

I knew little about Gong Gong's time in the army until 2015, when he and several other former soldiers from Force 136 were awarded medals for their bravery from the government of Taiwan. I had searched his name online one day, looking for a picture of one of his fisheries books, when I came across an oral history interview with Gong Gong that I didn't know existed, recorded in 2005 and archived online on the website of the National Archives of Singapore. Since I mostly only hear him speaking English and Hakka, it was the first time I'd ever really listened to him speaking Mandarin at length. To my surprise, I could understand most of the first few minutes of the recording. 'Wǒ de zǔfù, dàgài shì 1901 nián, chàbùduō yībǎi nián qián, dào nàbiān qù, dào Shāndǎgēn qù,' Gong Gong says. *It was about 1901, almost one hundred years ago, that my grandfather came to Sandakan*. When the interview turns to the specifics of his military training and service, I can't quite follow, but I keep listening anyway. His voice is soft and melodic.

Every night at the old house, Gong Gong watched TV until after we all went to bed. We waved goodnight to him one by one, each of us falling asleep to the faint murmurs of the Cantonese news and the whirring ceiling fan. I slept in the room next door, where bookshelves held endless piles of Mum's old schoolbooks and comics, the paper on the spines beginning to peel off at the edges: *Wuthering Heights, Sense and Sensibility, Asterix, Peanuts* and *The Famous Five.* Above and below were rows of Gong Gong's glass vials and jars, where tiny fish specimens were suspended in pale gold liquid. I could never look at them too closely. In the dark I thought I could feel their little silver eyes on me. Just before dawn, when the call to prayer from the blue mosque echoed over Likas Bay, I watched shades of deep blue light reflecting off the glass jars and the slender fish with their pearlescent scales. The prayer's floating melody seemed to falter in moments, suddenly far away, then returning again, high and clear, perhaps carried closer to us on the ocean wind. Meanwhile, the house began to slowly wake: lamps flickering on, footsteps shuffling, the sound of the kettle being set to boil.

3. *unripe-mango green*
As we got older, our visits to Kota Kinabalu became less frequent. Gong Gong didn't speak to us much, because we were kids; we didn't speak to him because he was old. Po Po spoke to us, with a mix of Hakka and a little bit of English, though mostly Hakka. Sara could understand

Hakka, although she couldn't speak it, but I couldn't understand it at all. We didn't speak back.

Back then I never thought to try and talk to Gong Gong and Po Po properly, beyond the warm chit-chat of *'how are you?'* and *'you've grown so tall!'* and *'there's been so much rain'*. I think it's because Po Po and Gong Gong had simply always been there, always the same, always in the same house with the same yellow flame tree by the door, their warm, wrinkled palms held against my cheeks. Always the same smells in the old house, always the same light. The house was like an untouchable archive of our early childhood – and my mother and aunt and uncle's childhoods – that would simply always be there.

In the years before Po Po died, I started to realise she knew much more English than I thought. She preferred Hakka, of course, and Hakka was the language of the household. So we stayed quiet – or we shut ourselves in the upstairs bedrooms with our Game Boys and *Harry Potter* books and CD players while the grown-ups downstairs chatted loudly in a foreign language, the language of the living room, the language of the dining table.

But in the kitchen, and in the back garden outside the kitchen window, language was less crucial. We sat on the concrete watching Po Po take the washing off the line, little green fruits swaying in the branches of the mango tree as the clouds darkened and the wind picked up. We sat cross-legged facing the long grass, Jackie the guard dog watching us wearily from where she sat curled by the front door. We watched the grass closely for lizards and threw crispy dried peas at each other, trying to catch them in our melamine cups. The white egret landed silently at the far end of the yard.

Six years ago, just after my first poetry pamphlet was published, we spent Christmas in Kota Kinabalu. It's strange to occupy a space as an adult where you feel like you'll perpetually be a child. Everything seems smaller than it should be. Sitting at the table, Mum motioned for me to give Po Po the copy of my book that I'd brought for her. On the inside cover I'd messily written my name for her in Chinese. She smiled and gazed at the cover, tracing the letters of the title with her forefinger, mouthing the words to me. Then she opened the book and flicked through the pages, murmuring occasional words: *flower*, *cloud*, *New Zealand*.

My inner geography of the house and its surroundings is hazy, informed purely by childhood memories. I couldn't draw you a map of the place, or tell you exactly how far it is to the sea; only that in the car I always knew once we reached the mosque on the corner we weren't far from home. My markers of the boundaries of this place were the blue coastline, the swimming pool on the hill, and the mountain. Recently, I felt a strong urge to go back and painstakingly redraw the lines of this landscape that lives in my memory before the physical traces disappeared altogether. The pieces repeat in my head like a spell. A kitchen, a swimming pool, a mountain.

4. *granite grey*

The mountain is hidden behind clouds for many hours of the day, but it's always there. I could sometimes see it in the mornings before the mist descended, its strange granite peaks like crooked teeth touching the sky.

It is made of molten rock pushed up through the earth's crust ten million years ago. Its granite core is igneous rock, crystallised magma. And the mountain is still slowly rising, uplifting at a rate of 5mm per year, thought to be caused by a slow process of subduction in the earth's crust. One hundred thousand years ago, during the Ice Age, Mount Kinabalu was coated in sheets of ice. Glaciers cut deep channels in the rock, carving out valleys and ravines.

Today, Mount Kinabalu stands at an elevation of 4,095 metres and is home to an estimated 5,000 to 6,000 plant species, with a high concentration found only on the mountain and nowhere else, including the Bornean black shrew, the Bornean ferret-badger, and the green Bornean spiderhunter bird. The World Wildlife Fund classifies Kinabalu's montane alpine forests as 'globally outstanding' because of its rich biodiversity; the only other Indo-Pacific ecoregion granted this status is the Eastern Himalayan broadleaf forests. There are approximately seven hundred and fifty orchid species found on the mountain; among them, the rare and sought-after Rothchild's slipper orchid, *Paphiopedilum rothschildianum*, which grows only at high elevations.

Kinabalu National Park was established in 1964, but this didn't stop rapid deforestation encroaching onto parts of Kinabalu's rainforests in the 1980s and '90s, mostly for logging and palm oil production. In 2000 the park was designated a World Heritage Site, and tourism boomed. Strict regulations and expensive climbing permits were introduced and, as a result, the indigenous Kadazan and Dusun people lost the ability to freely access their sacred ancestral mountain. Only in 2010 did Sabah Parks allocate one day a year for local Dusun people to undertake an annual pilgrimage to climb the mountain and perform traditional rituals to honour the dead.

The first European settlers and explorers gazed up at the mountain in awe. On a scientific expedition with the

Royal Society in 1961, the botanist E.J.H. Corner wrote of Mount Kinabalu's impressive peaks: 'Castellated, clouded, then sunlit and glittering with refreshed streams, the mountain presides over the landscapes of western North Borneo, beckoning the adventurer.' The mountain's history is inseparable from Borneo's history of European trade and colonisation, which began in the late 1700s with attempts by the Dutch to settle parts of Borneo. In 1812, the British East India Company attempted to seize control of ports but failed, and the project was deemed too expensive and risky – the island and its surrounding waters were too hostile, too wild. But in 1842, land in Sarawak was given to the British adventurer James Brookes, who established 'the Raj of Sarawak', his own monarchy and independent state. Brookes acquired further land for the British, clearing the way for the formation of British North Borneo in 1888, a new British protectorate administered by the North Borneo Chartered Company. Between 1880 and 1900, the British encouraged immigration of Hakka labourers from Guangdong to North Borneo to help boost economic growth. Among these labourers was Gong Gong's grandfather, who immigrated in 1901.

Japanese troops were met with little resistance when they landed on the island of Borneo in January 1942. Though British North Borneo had its own police force, there was no navy or army designated to protect it from invasion. Jesselton, present-day Kota Kinabalu, quickly surrendered, and the whole region became the territory of the Empire of Japan. Two large prisoner of war camps were set up on the island to detain British and Australian soldiers captured during the Battle of Singapore. A memorial now stands at Ranau, near the foothills of Kinabalu, where prisoners were forced to march from Sandakan to Kota Kinabalu along the eastern slopes of the mountain, over two hundred kilometres away. I've visited the memorial twice, once in the rainy season, once in the dry season. Half hidden at the top of a set of stone steps, a terraced peace garden has been planted with native Australian and English plants and flowers. Pale yellow roses and scarlet bottlebrush trees grow on the hillside overlooking rice paddies and banana trees.

By the time the Japanese surrendered in August 1945, the island of Borneo lay in devastation, all major cities and airports bombed. The North Borneo Chartered Company could not afford the cost of rebuilding infrastructure, and in 1946 handed over administration of the region to the British government. North Borneo remained a Crown colony until 1963, with the formation of the Federation of Malaysia. Today, the island is divided between three countries: Malaysia, Brunei and Indonesia.

Mount Kinabalu had been mapped and traversed by indigenous people for many generations before Hugh Low became the first white man to reach the summit in 1841. European naturalists relied heavily on the local people's knowledge of the land, but because the mountain was untouched by Western science it was regarded as wild, 'aboriginal'. Following Hugh Low, a flurry of European scientists and explorers arrived over the next fifty years, including the horticultural collector James Herbert Veitch in 1877, the zoologist John Whitehead in 1887, and insect collector J. Waterstradt in 1908. In 1910, Lilian S. Gibbs became the first European woman and the first botanist recorded to have reached the summit. Two landmark Royal Society expeditions took place in 1961 and 1964; my grandfather was present on one of these missions, collecting and cataloguing samples of freshwater fish from the mountain streams.

I made plans to follow in his footsteps on the mountain, to write about the waterfalls and other small bodies of water that Gong Gong studied, and to bring with me Lilian S. Gibbs' botanical notes. I booked a climbing permit and reserved a room at the lodge near the summit, where we would stay overnight and rise before dawn to reach Low's Peak at sunrise. I bought a waterproof parka, thermal leggings, a nylon backpack cover. As the news steadily unravelled, and so did our travel plans, I found myself clinging for as long as I could to the idea of walking up into the mist, spotting orchids, touching the cold granite summit and then, afterwards, sitting at the table with Gong Gong to tell him about the journey.

The news headlines repeat themselves in my head. For months I've been collecting them like field notes. 16th March: *'Malaysia will shut its borders to travellers, restrict internal movement, close schools and universities.'* 9th May: *'Malaysian borders remain closed to foreigners.'* 11th September: *'The government has decided to allow permanent residents, as well as foreign spouses of Malaysian citizens, to enter Malaysia, provided it is a one-way journey.'*

5. *formalin gold*
According to MountKinabalu.com, the climb takes a day and a half and is possible for 'anyone that is reasonably fit and healthy', even someone without any mountain-climbing experience, like me. I thought that if I could summit the mountain, I might come away with a deeper connection to the place where my mother was born. I couldn't let go of the mountain, even if I couldn't fathom how to write about it without being able to set foot on it or touch it. I reached for my copy of *The Living Mountain* by Nan Shepherd, a book unique in that it is not about reaching a summit, but instead closely traces the contours and colours of a mountain, its light, its air.

A line from Robert Macfarlane's introduction leapt out at me: 'to aim for the highest point is not the only way to climb a mountain'.

One way to climb a mountain, when travel is not possible, is to enter the archive. At the top of the steps of the Linnean Society of London, I ring a brass bell next to the door and hear its buzzing echo on the other side. The door is so heavy that I have to heave it open with my whole body. I tell the receptionist I have an appointment at the library and she waves me upstairs. Gold-framed portraits of distinguished white men line the walls above the carpeted stairs, along with cabinets displaying old pressed flowers.

I haven't set foot in a library in six months. Before the pandemic altered the shape of our daily lives, I spent half the week working in a library and archive dedicated to poetry. I breathlessly tell this to the young librarian, who has already set my stack of requested items on the table in front of me. I have just entered the most beautiful library I've ever seen, though I don't say this to the librarian, who probably hears it several times a day. He retreats to his office, leaving me with my shaky hands, my sharpened pencils and my pile of books.

I look around slowly, trying to take it all in. The walls are painted a soothing shade of mossy green, the colour of flax leaves from back home. Rickety ladders are fixed to the bookshelves, both down here and up on the mezzanine floor, where fluted columns with ornately curled tops touch the high ceilings. Soft sunlight filters through the floral-patterned skylights. I am alone in this intricate room, apart from several busts of old men and an enormous python skin coiled inside a glass case behind me. It's quiet apart from distant sounds of the city outside the arched windows. I can feel my heartbeat thumping in my ears. Titles of books, old and new, catch my eye: *Ancient Oaks of the English Landscape*; *AMERICAN SNAKES*; *The Flower of Empire*.

Earlier, I had waited with a small group of keen gallery visitors outside the gates of the Royal Academy. A woman with wispy white hair had seen me peering impatiently through the iron bars. She told me the gates would open at exactly quarter to eleven, in ten minutes' time. I'd been about to ask her if she had come for the Gauguin exhibition, when she said: 'I've just seen a bird of prey.'

I followed the line of her gaze through the gates towards the courtyard. 'It's gone,' she murmured. She said she'd seen the large dark-winged bird perch momentarily on the arm of a statue. She straightened her shoulders and held out her arm, mimicking the statue's pose, gesturing with her other hand to show me just where the bird had been. She laughed in amazement. I laughed with her and we looked up at the clear sky above the ornate rooftops, the blue so brilliant and cloudless we shielded our eyes.

With most of the city inaccessible to me until recently, it's been so long since I've set foot in an institution like this; one established almost solely for the cataloguing and archiving of Empire. In London, as with other European cities, I can feel the weight of a city built on the spoils of slavery and colonial violence. The Linnean Society is housed inside Burlington House, along with the Royal Academy of Arts and the Royal Astronomical Society, among other scientific institutions. Burlington House was owned by Lord Burlington, who purchased it in 1667, while he was Lord Treasurer of Ireland. Now, of course, the Linnean Society's focus has shifted to presenting and collecting important research on conservation and climate change. Libraries and archives may intend to exist outside of politics, with purely academic or research-related aims, but the archive is an institution and is therefore political. As the American writer and scholar Saidiya Hartman writes, when I step into this room, I must confront 'the authority of the archive and the limits it sets on what can be known, whose perspective matters'. This room is beautiful, but I feel the weight of its history.

The church bells chime softly to signal eleven o'clock. Noises of Piccadilly Circus fade into the background as I take out my notebook and place it on the desk next to two books pulled from the stack in front of me: *The Fresh-Water Fishes of North Borneo* by Robert F. Inger and Chin Phui Kong, my grandfather; and a volume of the *Linnean Society Journal* from 1914, bound in dark green leather with gold lettering stamped on the spine.

I open the blue book and there he is, sitting front and centre in a photograph of the Borneo Zoological Expedition team, from 1956, the same year my mum was born. I don't remember seeing this picture before; I've never seen him so young. Yet the shape of his face is just the same. I take a picture of the page with my phone and send it to Mum on WeChat. She responds minutes later to say she knows this picture well. She says the man seated next to Gong Gong – Dr Robert Inger, a herpetologist from Chicago – was Uncle Bob.

I've always known Gong Gong was an expert on fish in the North Borneo region, but I never knew what this really meant. I didn't know what he actually did. When I looked at this book when I was a girl, I only looked at the pictures. This time, I read slowly through Gong Gong's detailed accounts of Sabah's smallest bodies of water: streams, pools, waterfalls. In the book, each body of water is separated into its composite layers: the surface layer, upper strata, mid-water and low layer. And every fish specimen is described in minute detail, from the tip of the snout to the end of the opercular flap, the depth of the body, the diameter of the eye, the number of scales, the tiny distance between each fin. A series of black-and-white photographs show various riverbanks, pools and streams that served as the scientists' main collection sites. One photo shows vines and leaves tangled above a stream caught in a ray of sunlight, causing the surface of the water to shimmer. I can almost see the light vibrating.

The Fresh-Water Fishes of North Borneo was originally published in 1964; this printing from 1990 includes a new chapter written by my grandfather, listing further new fish species collected from Kinabalu National Park: 'A big room in the Department's head-quarters [. . .] was set aside for storage and display of fish specimens, preserved in formalin, in candy jars.' I think of the bedroom in the old house where I always slept as a child, with its sets of shelves dotted with golden jars and the tiny pink and silver fish suspended inside.

6. *mountain rhododendron red*
Alone in the empty library, I am submerged in the flora and waterways of Mount Kinabalu. It's strange to think that if my trip hadn't been cancelled, if borders around

the world hadn't been closed, I never would have spent so much time with my grandfather's book, here in this quiet archive dedicated to science.

I turn next to the dark green book, volume 42 of the *Linnean Society Journal*. I rest it on the special archival cushion on the desk in front of me, careful not to strain its spine, and use the satin-covered weights to hold the pages open.

Lilian S. Gibbs was born in London in 1870 and was educated at private schools in England and Europe. Described by John H. Beaman as 'a lady of independent means', she enrolled in Swanley Horticultural College in 1899 and later studied botany at the Royal College of Science. Employed by the British Museum for most of her life, Gibbs became known for her work on mountain ecosystems. She travelled widely on her plant-collecting missions, to Iceland, Zimbabwe, New Zealand, Australia, Fiji, Indonesia, Malaysia and South America. In 1905 she was elected as a Fellow of the Linnean Society of London, only a year after the society first began admitting women. In 1914, four years after becoming the first botanist and first European woman to summit Mount Kinabalu, she published an account of her observations titled 'A Contribution to the Flora and Plant Formations of Mount Kinabalu and the Highlands of British North Borneo' in the *Linnean Society Journal*.

I long to be able to see the plants and flowers of the rainforest more clearly, and her account gives me exactly this: a detailed catalogue, not a travelogue, listing plant textures, colours, measurements and Latin names of plant species at every stage of the climb. Like my grandfather's mapping of the different layers within a body of water, Gibbs outlines the composite layers of the mountain's rich ecosystem: secondary forest, primary high forest, mossy forest, scrub formation, low sheltered forest, sub-summit dwarf forest and the granite core.

In December 1909, Gibbs landed in Kota Kinabalu, then known as Jesselton. Beset by constant heavy rain, Gibbs and her small party of guides, porters and collecting assistants – most of them indigenous Dusun people – did not begin their climb from the foothill villages of Kiau until several weeks later, in January 1910. Her assistants, mostly teenage boys from nearby villages who knew the mountain well, helped her press plant samples and keep them dry as they made their way up through the wet rainforest. Mosses, rhododendrons and pitcher plants lined the trail. Gibbs spied one yellow and one red rhododendron growing side by side, but couldn't collect samples without the help of her local guide: 'The position of the Rhododendron was perilous, but Lamat proved equal to the occasion and brought me specimens of both species.'

The trees grew smaller and more sparse as they climbed into colder air. She turned her attention more closely to the mosses and orchids of the undergrowth. Prior to making the ascent to the summit, a sacrificial ritual was required in order to calm the spirits of the mountain – a ritual still practised by the Dusun community today – involving the slaughter of six chickens. On 22nd February, 1909, Gibbs neared the summit, climbing over rocky terrain up into the wind. The party paused to rest below the high forest and used water from pitcher plants for their tea. She kept her eyes low as the vegetation thinned, examining the mosses and tangled shrubs. Powerful winds had swept the dwarfed trees and their branches close against the surface of the rock over time. In a photograph of this part of the trail, the trees resemble the finely sculpted bonsai of Japanese gardens. They stopped near a sheltered stream overnight, where bright pink rhododendrons bloomed between slabs of rock. Leaving the others, Gibbs headed alone upstream to examine two deep pools and a low waterfall, where she collected moss from the rocks.

In the morning, sun broke through the trees and half of the party continued on to Low's Peak. At the edge of the dwarf forest, moss gave way to granite. The only plants: little yellow orchids growing in a slender chain, *Dendrochilum stachyodes*. She pocketed her specimen. Taking the hand of one of her guides to help keep her steady on the steep slope, they ran together up to the peak – this being one of the locals' preferred ways of negotiating difficult terrain. Breathless, they stopped at the point where the track ended. An icy waterfall cut through the rock at shoulder-level. She crouched low to touch the tiny plants growing in the cracks. She found a clump of small white flowers, *Drapetes ericoides*, and they reminded her suddenly of New Zealand.

In preparation for this trip I thought I would take, I had scrolled through endless pictures of the mountain's summit. I'd watched multi-part YouTube videos, read travel blogs, followed eco-tourism Instagram accounts. I imagined over and over again what it would be like to reach the summit; I was mostly anxious about whether I'd make it at all, worried my body would be too numb and exhausted, or too nauseous from the altitude. Lilian Gibbs' photographs of the summit, taken a century earlier, look almost identical to contemporary images: a grey moonscape of dark valleys of rock encircled by cloud. In the library, I lean close to examine all the intricate ridges and striations in the granite, easily visible in the black-and-white image. The curved shape of Low's Peak rises into the sky like a tidal wave.

Up there, Gibbs found herself alone, the rest of the party taking shelter from the wind further down the path. She stood still, watching clouds roll over 'the mighty abyss' below. She examined the granite plateau in intense detail, as if it might have been an orchid or a bed of moss, committing to memory its slopes, its ridges and textures:

> Huge peaks, almost all of the same height, align themselves on its surface like the columns of some roofless titanic temple, recalling the dissected plateaus of Skye . . .

One thing many climbers note about Mount Kinabalu's summit is the wind: icy, biting, whistling. Gibbs felt it, 'the cold wind whistling through the gap' between jagged rocks. Along with the others, she wrote her name down on a slip of paper, put it inside a glass bottle, nestled the bottle against the slope and built a small cairn of stones to protect it.

Accounts written by colonial botanists and naturalists are both fascinating and uncomfortable. Gibbs makes plain the importance of botanical study in exploiting North Borneo's 'natural riches' to ensure the region's success as a colony. She repeatedly praises the locals' 'industrious' nature and 'commercial spirit', while at the same time observing the destruction wrought by colonial expansion on their livelihoods. But this colonial history is part of what has shaped me. It was the British who encouraged migration from southern China to Borneo in the early 1900s, creating settlements of Hakka labourers in Sabah, where Hakka people now make up the majority of the Chinese community.

These days, no visitor is permitted to leave any item behind on the summit of Mount Kinabalu, or anywhere along the trail. It is sacred land. Though the highest peak was named for the first Englishman to conquer it, the mountain does not belong to him. It never did.

7. *butterfly-wing blue*
My grandfather and Lilian Gibbs were both scientists, unlike me. I read their descriptions without always understanding the words they use. They went to the mountain to build a catalogue of plants and fishes and streams, and now, reading their work, I begin to build a catalogue of colours.

Red is the colour of mountain rhododendrons and tiny orchids. The 'reddish in colour and red-veined' *Styphelia learmonthiana* is one of Gibbs' plant specimens held at the Herbarium at Kew Gardens, which has been digitised online. She saw this plant just below the summit of Mount Kinabalu, exposed to the wind, growing up between cracks in the granite. She had never seen it before and took out her pencil and notebook to sketch its intricate shape: bursts of tiny white petals all tightly cupped by the dark pink sepal, the part of the stem that holds the flower head.

In the digitised image of her specimen, the plant is fixed to a sheet of yellowed paper, along with a card giving its name and where it was collected ('British North Borneo, Kinabalu, 1910'). Her handwritten words are compressed, made up of loose curls, as if quickly scrawled. The stems are thin and fragile now. The leaves and petals have faded to a dull gold, pressed against the page, all facing in one direction as if caught blowing in the wind of the peak. A small unfolded envelope is fixed to the sheet, opening outwards like an advent calendar window, where a handful of dried seeds has been kept safe.

My first summer in London, I picked up a copy of *Werner's Nomenclature of Colours* at the gift shop of the Natural History Museum. Published in 1814, the book is a taxonomy of colour descriptions in reference to specific animals, vegetables and minerals. Abraham Gottlob Werner was a German geologist who first set about classifying crystals by colour. The book's charts are divided into whites, greys, blacks, blues, purples, greens, yellows, oranges, reds, browns. For each shade, he gives three examples of the colour spotted in the natural world. When describing certain shades of blue, Werner looked to the edges of butterfly wings, as I do. *Ultramarine Blue* is the colour of the 'Upper Side of the Wings of small blue Heath Butterfly'; *Flax-flower Blue* is the 'Light Parts of the Margin of the Wings of Devil's Butterfly'.

Werner's Nomenclature of Colours reads like a colonial archive of colour. Werner sought 'to remove the present confusion in the names of colours' and establish a standardised colour naming system for use among naturalists, collectors and painters, at a time when scientists accompanied colonists on their voyages to the far reaches of the British Empire, like Sir Joseph Banks bringing Aotearoa's plant specimens home on the *Endeavour*. Within this book, Charles Darwin found a new language for describing colour; he used it to help keep a record of his journey on the HMS *Beagle* to Australia, New Zealand, Tahiti and South America from 1831 to 1836.

But there is no standard catalogue of colour names. Our language for colours shifts according to our own experiences and memories: the blue of a giant Borneo butterfly's wings pinned in a glass case; the yellow at the centre of a custard tart. These colours are changing all the time.

8. *myrtle flower pale pink*
An afternoon of warm rain on the foothills of Mount Kinabalu, in 1910. I see her in her white cotton dress,

bending low to touch the leaves of a shrub with pink blooms. She recognises it immediately: *Anisophyllea*. She stops. The smell, the colour. She recalls suddenly a valley in Rotorua, New Zealand, where she had trekked alone five years earlier under the hard sun. This plant had thrived there in the wind. On the same slope she recognises a clump of myrtle, *Baeckea frutescens*, a tree of healing. She crushes the end of a needle-like leaf between her fingers and takes in the scent. This is her language: the language of plants at high altitudes.

A day of unrelenting sun in June, 1964. My grandfather crouches in the shade by the flowing stream, his khaki trousers rolled up just above his ankles. He watches the surface closely, reading the patterns of movement in the water. A few metres downstream, the torrent narrows where water tumbles over large rocks. As they wait in silence for fish to rise to the surface, he can hear the sound of the waterfall coursing into a larger body of water below.

A bright morning in September, 2020: I am sitting alone in the library with flax-green walls. This library is a library of the British Empire and all its flora, fauna and indigenous peoples. I think of my own natural history, both sides of my heritage rooted in island colonies. On the desk in front of me, two black-and-white photographs side by side: one shows the granite rock face of Kinabalu's summit, taken in 1910. The other, from 1956, of the crystal-still surface of a stream in the Sabah rainforest, a pattern of leaves and tangled vines reflected on the surface, almost moving.

9. *dandelion yellow*

The shape of my world is altered now. It's easy to feel stranded, stuck, no longer on the path I'd planned. There's talk of this year marking the end of long-haul travel and it's true, travel is a luxury. When I think of all the places I can't reach that I wish I could reach, I feel a burning guilt in me. But there are so many of us whose skin, whose lineage, is split along lines of migration.

Whenever my mum meets someone new who is Hakka just like her, her eyes light up. She'll say to me warmly, 'they're Hakka too!' and I'll smile and nod, pretending I know what this really means. I know what the language sounds like, or at least the variant of Hakka that my family speaks, which is as familiar to me as the sound of the sea, but I can't understand it. I know there are special Hakka delicacies, rich-smelling braised dishes of tofu, pork and offal, but I didn't grow up with them. If I can't speak the language or cook any of the recipes, I've never felt sure that I could claim this ancestral link.

Hakka isn't an ethnicity, but a distinct cultural subgroup of the Han Chinese majority. The history of my ancestors is a history of migration, displacement and transience. First from northern and central China, from where we are thought to have originated, down to southern China and Taiwan. Then, huge waves of migration from the 1850s onwards, as a result of land disputes, famines and upheaval – to Malaysia, where my grandparents fled, to Singapore, Vietnam, India, North and South America, the Caribbean, Europe, Australia, Aotearoa and other lands. I now understand that being Hakka means we don't all come from one place, but rather, from scattered villages and scattered islands. It means we don't all speak one language, but many regional variants of multiple languages, including English.

I remember looking up the Mandarin word for Hakka on my phone during one of my first Chinese classes at university – 客家人, kèjiā rén. The literal English translation of the phrase popped up underneath: *guest people*. I never felt the significance of the meaning of these words until years later. What does it mean to be a guest in Aotearoa: part coloniser, part recent migrant? What does it mean to be a guest in Britain under a popular government-led campaign of anti-migrant rhetoric and policy? As the Aotearoa writer K. Emma Ng asks: 'How can we belong here, become "from here", without re-enacting the violence that is historically embedded in the gesture of trying to belong?' It begins somewhere in acknowledging that both my whiteness and my Chineseness are immigrant identities. It begins with understanding what it means to put down roots on stolen land, and doing so with intention, with care and respect. It means collective responsibility, and working towards a better world for indigenous and displaced people.

In Aotearoa we have an important word for this: tauiwi. Non-Māori, non-indigenous. Some New Zealanders can't face being called a *guest* – they can't see themselves as foreign, nor our grandfathers and great-grandfathers who drew lines along the land belonging to tangata whenua. But being tauiwi doesn't mean I'm left drifting, rootless, untethered to an ancestral homeland. It means tracing the threads back to the roots of my history, my colonial history, and holding all the pieces in my hands. It means always looking for the sea.

A well-known metaphor for the Hakka people is the dandelion – the sunny yellow flower that grows like a weed. The food writer Linda Lau Anusasananan writes in *The Hakka Cookbook:* 'Like a dandelion, a Hakka can land anywhere, take root in the poorest soil, and flourish and flower.' In traditional Chinese medicine, the dandelion, like other bitter-tasting plants, is used for cleansing and healing. Bright dandelions grew all over the grass by the school buildings in Wellington. We used to pick them and crush the petals between forefinger and thumb, staining our fingers yellow.

10. *magpie tailfeather blue*
During the long, anxious summer, I taught myself how to sew. I had a piece of Indonesian indigo cotton given to me by my mother, folded away at the back of my wardrobe. It reminded me of pieces of a handmade patchwork quilt I had when I was little, given to me by Po Po and Gong Gong. It was made from scraps of patterned fabrics – I remember a row of sailboats, gold stars and clouds – bordered by soft turquoise brushed cotton that was beginning to wear away underneath. Mum knew where all the squares of fabric had come from: dresses that Po Po had worn, curtains, pyjamas that had been outgrown. I'd always assumed this was Po Po's handiwork, and never thought to find out more – until one day I told Mum I'd been learning to sew, and she sent back a message that read: 'Gong Gong made those quilts on that old sewing machine next to the piano, you know.' I stopped, wondering how I'd never known this before. There were several quilts: at least three, one for each of his older grandchildren. Each one an archive made of cloth, held together by seams sewn before I was born, folded into a box and carried across the sea.

My grandparents' house always felt like an archive of sorts – not one left dusty and untouched, but a living record of a scattered family. At this moment we don't know when we'll see each other again, but it doesn't always matter. This is an archive rooted in memory, and in our shared habit of collecting things and never throwing them away.

A personal archive of the colour blue: Wellington harbour beneath dark clouds; the wide wings of a *Tanaecia iapis* butterfly pinned in a glass case; the iridescent tail feathers of a magpie lying with its head turned gracefully to one side, as if asleep on the footpath; a hundred-year-old pressed orchid specimen collected from Borneo, the veins of its curled petals still purple and indigo; a petrol-blue enamel pot that once belonged to Po Po; my mother's deep sea blue sewing box; a swimming pool surrounded by rainforest hills.

'A place becomes a home when it sustains you, when it feeds you in body as well as spirit,' Robin Wall Kimmerer writes in *Braiding Sweetgrass*. I think of the last bodies of water I have touched sustaining me, connecting me to places I can't reach. In midsummer, under heavy clouds off the coast of Kent, near the strip of water that separates this small island from the continent of Europe. Late summer, in a river near Oxford, where David swam out to the other side to pick blackberries and carried them back across the water to me with one hand held above him. Early autumn in the darkening pond, leaves falling around me and from me as I pulled my aching body up the metal ladder, squeezing pond water from my hair. I think of my untidy balcony garden, a collection of plants placed there to help sustain both my body and spirit: ginger, garlic, spring onions, mint, marigolds.

Outside my window, the little kōwhai grows steadily in its pot, its leaves turning dark and strong.

Notes

The Safe Zone

Kyo Maclear. *Birds Art Life: A Year of Observation*. New York: Scribner, 2017.

Rena Priest. 'What Happens to Them Happens to Us'. *Hakai Magazine*, 12 May 2020: <https://www.hakaimagazine.com/features/what-happens-to-them-happens-to-us/>.

John Ristau. 'Ghost quakes: The ghost chips of earthquakes'. *Newshub NZ*, 10 September 2018: <https://newshub.co.nz/home/newzealand/2018/08/ghost-quakes-the-ghost-chips-of-earthquakes.html>.

Where the Kōwhai Blooms

Joseph Banks' Florilegium: Botanical Treasures from Cook's First Voyage. London: Thames & Hudson, 2017 (first published 1990).

Walter Reginald Brook Oliver. *Botanical Discovery in New Zealand: The Visiting Botanists*. Wellington: Hutcheson, Bowman & Stewart, 1951.

Joseph Angus Mackay. *Historic Poverty Bay and the East Coast, North Island, New Zealand*. Gisborne: J.A. Mackay, 1949.

'Sophora Tetraptera. Winged-Podded Sophora'. *Curtis's Botanical Magazine*, 1791.

Anna Jackson. *Diary Poetics: Form and Style in Writers' Diaries, 1915–1962*. Oxford: Routledge, 2010.

Sylvia Plath. *The Bell Jar*. London: Faber & Faber, 2001 (1963).

Franny Choi. 'How to Let Go of the World'. *PEN America*, 3 October 2019: <https://pen.org/how-to-let-go-of-the-world/>.

Katherine Mansfield. 'At the Bay', from *The Garden Party and Other Stories*. London: Penguin Books, 1997 (1922).

Jessica J. Lee. *Turning*. London: Virago, 2017.

Quentin Pope (ed.). *Kowhai Gold: An Anthology of Contemporary New Zealand Verse*. London: J.M. Dent & Sons, 1930.

The Language of Waves

Pliny the Elder. *The Complete Works of Pliny the Elder*. East Sussex: Delphi Classics, 2015.

Abi Andrews. *The Word for Woman Is Wilderness*. London: Serpent's Tail, 2018.

Cheryl Strayed. *Wild*. London: Atlantic Books, 2012.

Abi Palmer. *Sanatorium*. London: Penned in the Margins, 2020.

Kirstie Millar *Curses, Curses*. London: Takeaway Press, 2019.

Crushed Little Stars

Mitski. *Bury Me at Makeout Creek*. New York: Double Double Whammy Records, 2014.

Mitski. *Puberty 2*. Indiana: Dead Oceans, 2016.

Aleyna Martinez. Tayi Tibble on Poūkahangatus & Decolonising the Mind. *Serum Digital Magazine*, 13 September 2018: <https://digital-serum.com/2018/09/13/author-tayi-tibble-on-poukahangatus-decolonising-the-mind/>

Will Harris. *Mixed-Race Superman*. London: Peninsula Press, 2018.

Talia Smith. *The heart is the strongest muscle in the body*. Auckland: Window Gallery, 2018: multimedia artwork accessible at <https://www.windowgallery.co.nz/exhibitions/the-heart-is-the-strongest-muscle-in-the-body>.

Michelle Zauner. 'Crying in H Mart'. *New Yorker*, 20 August 2018.

Layli Long Soldier. *Whereas*. Minneapolis: Graywolf Press, 2017.

Sarah Howe. *Loop of Jade*. London: Chatto & Windus, 2015.

Jem Yoshioka. *Visits*. 2017: <http://jemshed.com/2016/05/visits-and-habits/>.

Falling City

Eileen Chang. *Love in a Fallen City* (trans. by Karen S. Kingsbury). New York: NYRB Classics, 2006 (1943).

Robin Hyde. *Dragon Rampant*. Wanganui: AG Books, 2013.

Eileen Chang. *Half a Lifelong Romance* (trans. by Karen S. Kingsbury). New York: Anchor, 2016 (1948–50).

The Plum Rains

Du Fu. '梅雨' ('Plum Rains'), *The Poetry of Du Fu: Volume 1* (trans. and ed. by Stephen Owen). Berlin: De Gruyter, 2016.

Nina Li Coomes. 'What Miyazaki's Heroines Taught Me About My Mixed-Race Identity'. *Catapult*. 3 October 2016: <https://catapult.co/stories/fans-what-miyazakis-heroines-taught-me-about-my-mixed-race-identity>.

We Are All Dreaming of Swimming Pools

Leanne Shapton. *Swimming Studies*. New York: Blue Rider Press, 2012.

Ellena Savage. 'Everything Anyone Has Ever Said About the Pool'. *Kill Your Darlings*, 3 June 2019: < https://www.killyourdarlings.com.au/article/everything-anyone-has-ever-said-about-the-pool/>.

J.A. Johnson. *Assessing the Impact of Climate Change in Borneo*. Washington, D.C.: World Wildlife Fund's Environmental Economics Series, 14 June 2012.

Unpeel

Jane Wong. 'Offerings'. *The Common*, 19 June 2019: <https://www.thecommononline.org/offerings/>.

Faraway Love

Louise DeSalvo & Mitchell Alexander Leaska (eds). *The Letters of Vita Sackville-West to Virginia Woolf*. San Francisco: Cleis Press, 2001.

Katherine Mansfield. 'The Tiredness of Rosabel', from *Katherine Mansfield's Short Stories*. Auckland: Penguin Random House New Zealand, 2010 (1908).

Margaret Atwood. *The Handmaid's Tale*. New York: Anchor Books, 1998 (1985).

Emily Jungmin Yoon (ed.). *Against Healing: Nine Korean Poets (Translating Feminisms)*. London: Tilted Axis Press, 2019.

Tender Gardens

John MacKinnon and Karen Phillips. *A Field Guide to the Birds of China*. Oxford: Oxford University Press, 2020 (2000).

Alexander Chee. *How to Write an Autobiographical Novel*. London: Bloomsbury Publishing, 2018.

Emily Jungmin Yoon. *A Cruelty Special to our Species*. New York: Ecco Press, 2018.

Rachael Allen. *Kingdomland*. London: Faber & Faber, 2019.

Alison Wong. 'Pure Brightness'. *Griffith Review 43: Pacific Highways*, January 2014: < https://www.griffithreview.com/articles/pure-brightness/>.

Manying Ip (ed.). *Unfolding History, Evolving Identity: the Chinese in New Zealand*. Auckland: Auckland University Press, 2003.

Alison Wong. 'The River Bears Our Name', from *Cup*. Wellington: Steele Roberts, 2006.

Maraea Rakuraku & Vana Manasiadis (eds), *tātai whetū: seven Māori women poets in translation*. Wellington: Seraph Press, 2018.

Julia C. Lin (ed. and trans.). *Women of the Red Plain: An Anthology of Contemporary Chinese Women Poets*. New York: Puffin, 1993.

Bing Xin 冰心. '纸船' ('Paper Boats'), from 纸船: 传世经典美文 ('*Paper Boats: Classic Masterpieces*'). Fuzhou: Fujian People's Publishing House, 2012.

Ache

Ava Wong Davies, 'The First', from *At the Pond: Swimming at the Hampstead Ladies' Pond*. London: Daunt Books Publishing, 2019.

Jessica J. Lee. *Turning*. London: Virago, 2017.

Katherine Mansfield. 'At the Bay', from *The Garden Party and Other Stories*. London: Penguin Books, 1997 (1922).

Sharlene Teo. 'Echolocation', from *At the Pond: Swimming*

at the Hampstead Ladies' Pond. London: Daunt Books Publishing, 2019.

三点水

Ilaria Maria Sala. 'What the world's fascination with a female-only Chinese script says about cultural appropriation'. *Quartz*, 24 May 2018: <https://qz.com/1271372/what-the-worlds-fascination-with-nushu-a-female-only-chinese-script-says-about-cultural-appropriation/>.

Jen Bervin. *Su Hui's Reversible Poem*. Video installation (various dimensions) & two framed double-sided silk embroideries, 33 ½ x 20 ½ x 8 in.

Rainbow Chan. *To Enclose One's Mouth*. Installation at 4A Centre for Contemporary Asian Art, Sydney, 2017.

Kerry Ann Lee. *The Unavailable Memory of Gold Coin Café*. Limited edition exhibition catalogue designed, printed and produced by the artist, 2015: <https://enjoy.org.nz/media/uploads/2016_04/2015_TheUnavailableMemoryofGoldCoinCafe_KerryAnnLee.pdf>.

Guerrino Marsecano. *The English–Hakka Dictionary* 英客字典, 光啟出版社. 1959.

Tomoko Kawao. 「家」. 2014: < https://www.instagram.com/p/B-lmWgYnMFX/?utm_source=ig_web_copy_link>

Museum of White Clouds

Kerry Ann Lee. *Return to Skyland*. Video & vinyl wallpaper installation at the National Museum of New Zealand, Te Papa Tongarewa, 2018.

In the Archive of Waterfalls

Robert F. Inger and Phui Kong Chin. *The Fresh-Water Fishes of North Borneo*. Fieldiana: Zoology [vol. 45]. Sabah, Malaysia: Sabah Zoological Society, 1990 (1964).

E.J.H. Corner. *Royal Society Expedition to North Borneo 1961*. Special Reports: 1. SOILS, Linnean Society London, [vol. 175, iss. 1], January 1964.

Nan Shepherd. *The Living Mountain*. London: Canongate Books, 2011 (1977).

Saidiya Hartman. *Wayward Lives, Beautiful Experiments*. London: Serpent's Tail, 2019.

Lilian S. Gibbs. *A Contribution to the Flora and Plant Formations of Mount Kinabalu and the Highlands of British North Borneo*. Malaysia; London: Natural History Publications (Borneo) in association with The Linnean Society London, 2001.

Patrick Syme. *Werner's Nomenclature of Colours: Adapted to Zoology, Botany, Chemistry, Mineralogy, Anatomy, and the Arts*. London: Natural History Museum, 2017 (1814).

K. Emma Ng. *Old Asian, New Asian*. Wellington: Bridget Williams Books, 2017.

Linda Lau Anusasananan. *The Hakka Cookbook*. Berkley: University of California Press, 2012.

Robin Wall Kimmerer. *Braiding Sweetgrass: Indigenous Wisdom, Scientific Knowledge and the Teachings of Plants*. London: Penguin Books, 2020 (2013).

Thank you to the editors of the following publications where early versions of these essays first appeared: 'A Girl Swimming Is a Body of Water' in *The Willowherb Review* and *At the Pond*, published by Daunt Books Publishing; 'The Language of Waves' in *Ache Magazine*; 'Falling City' in *The Shanghai Literary Review* and *Magnolia, 木蘭*, published by Nine Arches Press; 'Unpeel' in AAWW's *The Margins*; 'Tender Gardens' in *Landfall*; 'Ache: A Swimming Diary' in *Turbine | Kapohau*; and 'Museum of White Clouds' in *Hainamana Arts*. 'Faraway Love' was originally commissioned by the e-newsletter series *close*.

Acknowledgements

I am forever grateful that I've formed friendships with a group of women whose art and activism constantly inspires me. Many of them read and helped shape early drafts of these essays: thank you to Saradha Soobrayen, Pema Monaghan, Pratyusha and Jennifer Wong.

This book would not exist without Jessica J. Lee, whose memoir *Turning* set me on my path and made this work feel possible. Thank you for your friendship and support, and for our cold swims.

In establishing the Nan Shepherd Prize, Canongate have helped make the field of nature writing more inclusive. I'm endlessly grateful for their vision and their support – especially my editor Megan Reid, Caroline Clarke, Vicki Rutherford, Alice Shortland and Lucy Zhou, and my brilliant copyeditor Saba Ahmed.

Thanks to my agent, Kirsty McLachlan, for her constant support, to Gill Heeley for her stunning painted artwork on the cover, and to Jo Dingley for her illustrations.

AKNOWLEDGEMENTS

Thanks also to Rose Lu, Helen Rickerby and Sarah Webster, whose words I always, always value. And to past writing teachers Marin Sardy, Ashleigh Young and Harry Ricketts, and my workshop classmates from both 2013 and 2020, who encouraged me to keep writing about whales.

I'm indebted to the librarians at the Linnean Society of London, my 书法 teacher at London Ming'Ai Institute, Hu Laoshi, and all my former colleagues at the National Poetry Library.

Thanks most of all to my family, especially Mum, Dad, Gong Gong and Po Po, for all those trips up Mount Kinabalu and to the Sabah Museum. Gong Gong, Kiu Kiu, Ai Lan, Aunty Bin, Uncle Boon, Sara, Adrian – I hope we'll all get to see each other again soon.

Thank you, David, for always accompanying me in search of the sea.